SPIRIT AND FORM

On the True Meaning of Individuality
and the Art of Psychological Sculpting

Benjamin M. Goldberg, Ph.D.

iUniverse, Inc.
Bloomington

Spirit and Form
On the True Meaning of Individuality and
the Art of Psychological Sculpting

iUniverse books may be ordered through booksellers or by contacting:

iUniverse
1663 Liberty Drive
Bloomington, IN 47403
www.iuniverse.com
1-800-Authors (1-800-288-4677)

Because of the dynamic nature of the Internet, any Web addresses or links contained in this book
may have changed since publication and may no longer be valid. The views expressed in this work
are solely those of the author and do not necessarily reflect the views of the publisher, and the
publisher hereby disclaims any responsibility for them.

ISBN: 978-1-4502-5251-5 (pbk)
ISBN: 978-1-4502-5252-2 (cloth)
ISBN: 978-1-4502-5253-9 (ebk)

Library of Congress Control Number: 2010912168

Printed in the United States of America

iUniverse rev. date: 10/18/10

For Margaret, Daniel, Gregory, and Ace

The Spirit, without moving, is swifter than the mind; the senses cannot reach him: he is ever beyond them. Standing still, he overtakes those who run.

Isha Upanishad

Contents

Preface

It is probably a truism of psychological theorizing that the theory itself, no matter how intellectual or abstruse, is fundamentally inseparable from the personal biography of the theoretician. Growing up with an austere and prominent father, it is not surprising that Sigmund Freud's psychology is decidedly paternalistic, whereas Carl Jung's, for contralateral reasons, is decidedly maternalistic. Alfred Adler was born with a club foot, and the central theme of his psychology is power and compensation for feelings of inferiority. Perhaps Harry Stack Sullivan's emphasis on interpersonalism reflects the isolation of a man of his era having to hide his sexuality. Speculation notwithstanding, it is hard to imagine that any theory of human nature and experience could *not* be infused with, and configured by, the contingencies of one's childhood.

In my own case, the themes of transcendent spiritualism and existential authenticity emerged from a compilation of definitive experiences and observations. As early as five years of age, and extending into my late twenties, I had a number of "peak experiences," as perfectly described and exemplified by Richard Bucke in his 1901 manuscript entitled *Cosmic Consciousness*. Similar to the phenomenological categorizations as put forth by William James, Alfred Tennyson, Meister Eckhart, William Blake, and D.T. Suzuki (to name but a few), the hallmark of the peak experience is ego transcendence, or the clear and immediate apprehension of the supreme identity of oneself with the Infinite. Ineffable to its core, this experience does not readily lend itself to linguistic and ideational representation, and is consequently ignored or irrelevant in a world of logical positivism. But I did not ignore it. Compared to the apparently bereft subjectivity of those who mechanically attended church and synagogue without a true evolution in their religious consciousness, the spiritual element of the peak experience was profound, compelling, joyous, and transformative. It carved itself into my psyche and affected me with no less turbulence than did the death of my father and the birth of my children.

Along with the experience and concept of transcendence and spirituality was the painstaking evolution of the notion of existential authenticity. Raised primarily by narcissistic caregivers who saw in me what they wanted to see, and accordingly encouraged and directed me on *their* terms, I knew the anxiety and confusion of self-anonymity, as I was hopelessly shrouded and peripheralized by the ideas, attitudes, and ambitions that were ascribed to me by others. To fulfill her own unfulfilled aspirations, my mother's expectation was that I would become a concert pianist, whereas my grandfather had me following in his footsteps by becoming a physician. Querying into my soul with the simple question, "What would *you* like to do?," apparently never entered their minds, or at least was not deemed sufficiently important. In terms of aptitudes and interests I had no knowledge of myself, except perhaps for vague intimations, and in the context of family dynamics I clearly understood Ralph Ellisons's metaphor of invisibility.

Burning with religious questions while annihilated in my own identity, I was now three semesters into my college career, majoring in pre-med, and with suffering grades. Calculus, chemistry, biology, and anatomy drew no interest from me, as I began to adumbrate the notions of existential alienation and spiritual impoverishment. With the peaking tension of personal crisis I quite incidentally picked up Herman Hesse's *Demian*, which was borrowed from a friend and for months had been sitting on my shelf under the dust of neglect. In a single sitting, in a single afternoon of utter hypnotic absorption, I read and completed this piece of literature, and as its last words were inscribed in my memory I had yet another, and perhaps the most intense, of my peak experiences. With an explosion of instantaneous insight I knew who I was, and proceeded immediately from Hesse to Jung, Freud, existentialism, phenomenology, and the religions and philosophies of the East. Perhaps it was synchronistic, or perhaps purely fortuitous, but my grandfather died a few weeks later, and I immediately switched my major to psychology, which was the premier significant decision of my life.

During the years of my doctoral work in psychology, the ineluctably regnant question of the nature of the conscious Self or Spirit was the cornerstone of my intellectual striving. My readings in Zen Buddhism helped me to appreciate that the nature of the Spirit cannot be conceptualized or otherwise objectively known, but that the dynamism of its *activity* can be apprehended *in vivo*. What else could possibly be the motif and movement of the Spirit other than an act of selfless love, and how else could this love be manifested but in the creation and perfection of the finite universe? And herein lay the synthesis of transcendent spiritualism and existential authenticity: the conscious Self or Spirit manifests itself in the act of cultivating individuality of form. Everything in my universe fell into its proper place.

Despite a morass of diverging theories concerning the etiology of human psychopathology and unhappiness, my subsequent experiences as a psychologist in private practice consistently underscored the impression that the bulk of the maladies I was encountering were the byproducts of petrifaction, or the absence of authentic, personal growth and evolution. Correlatively, the appropriate model of therapy should not substantively involve such principles as "changing" or "fixing," but rather the assertion that the intrinsic form of the individual is perfect unto itself, and thus needs to be discerned, released, and articulated. As there is no need for the violent principle of permutation, the aim of the therapeutic process must be akin to the art of sculpting in stone. The occlusive layers of extrinsic thoughts, feelings, ambitions, and self-assessments are to be "chipped away," or subtracted from the equation, like inchoate rock shrouding a statue or grime on a window, allowing the light of true form or individuality to be revealed and seek its course of outward expression.

Practically speaking, the empirical results of my body of theory and practice have been fruitful ones, for which I am immeasurably thankful. They are like jewels born of thirty-five years of thought, study, and intensive human engagement, embodied academically in *Spirit and Form*, my penultimate statement, and the veriest reflection of my soul.

I

Alienation and Individuation

A child's awe and wonder at life's simplicities carries the intimation that there is ultimately so much more, not less, to that which is the foundation or origin of these precious gifts. The finite somehow implies the Infinite, and reductionistic thinking is alien to the child's mind. Nothing is "just" this or "just" that, and the universe does not rest precariously on the head of a pin. It is grounded in Absolute Being, and the child seems to know this. The present moment is utterly replete in its splendor, and there is no thought of it being lost or diminished. The arctic wind of cynicism and negativity has yet to pierce the child's heart and mind, and she is joyously loved and sustained by all that surrounds her.

The age of innocence ends with the dawning of ego consciousness, as the child's awareness of self is gradually reduced to her physical organism and the spark of consciousness in her head. She is now but a speck of dust in an inestimably vast universe, one that she "encounters," as if the branch of a tree encounters the trunk from which it grows. The world that spawned her, that loves her as integral to itself, is divorced as the foundation of her being, and positioned in opposition to what remains of her. Far from being her very substratum, the universe is now hostile and wholly other, for in her state of nescience she cannot appreciate that as an ocean wave is a particular manifestation of the entire ocean, so it contains the entire ocean. Cosmologically speaking, she feels completely alone.

Although a subjectively vivid reality, this feeling of aloneness is an illusion. As a physical being, the human organism is inextricable from that which it calls its environment. The act of breathing, for example, as the symbol and most fundamental aspect of human life, cannot be described without a description of the oxygen and carbon dioxide entering and leaving the lungs. And if we are to describe the oxygen, we must include a description of the plants and trees producing this oxygen, the soil in which they grow, the rain that fertilizes the soil, the clouds that contain the rain, and the heavens that contain the clouds. In short, to render a comprehensive scientific description of a particular organism, one must include a description of the surface tension of a bubble in the Amazon River, and the gaseous pressure of some star light-years away. Naturally, this is completely impractical, so it is agreed that the description of the human organism will end with the epidermis. The problem is not with the convention, but with the almost inevitable tendency to *forget* that it is a convention - to take it seriously.

As psychological beings we thus see ourselves as sparks of consciousness residing in our heads, looking out at the world around us. Yet since consciousness does not occupy space, and is therefore spaceless and sizeless, it cannot be positioned at any particular point in space. We cannot say that consciousness is any more in our heads than that it is "out there" in the field of objects, for when we speak of spacelessness, terms such as "in," "out," and "around" no longer apply. The object in my field of view is indeed in or of my consciousness, but where is my consciousness? Phenomenologically, the tree in front of my house is in front of my house, yet as the result of electromagnetic activity transforming into the neurochemical activity of the sense organs and brain, it is also a state of my brain and nervous system. Moreover, mind, to a large degree, is socially constituted. The act of thinking is fundamentally the internalization of dialectical and didactic relationships with others, and our very concept and sense of self are predominantly configured by the self-reflections from our interactions with these others. From the standpoint of the physical and social sciences, we are alone neither in the universe nor in our skins.

Coming of age with the profound anxiety of existential alienation, the individual looks to allay this dread. In some instances she avoids it, losing herself in endless stimulation and distraction. In other instances she attempts to bolster herself against it by questing for power, status, and wealth, or zealously adopting some idea, principle, symbol, or cause that is transcendent, fixed, and permanent. The transcendent and permanent object par excellence is, of course, God, and the pious seek affinity with him. Yet how does one get "closer" to God when, because of his infinite status, one can never be away from him? Only finite objects can be proximal or distal in relation to oneself, and to think that one can approach or pull away from God is to deny him his infinity and set him at a distance, as just another finite object of knowledge. The attempt to get closer to God is not only impossible and unnecessary, but reinforces the very experience of separateness that generates this need for cultivated propinquity.

What, then, is one to do? What can one do? It seems that the only option is to accept oneself *as is*. Ultimately, this is a profound truth, but it can be misleading if our terms are imprecise. If by "as is" we mean a current and chronic state of internal impoverishment and situational unhappiness, such acceptance would be little more than an act of passive acquiescence to substandard conditions. The very spirit of life is extinguished in this equation. If accepting oneself "as is" means acknowledging and embracing one's true nature or authentic self, we then hold the remedy for existential alienation in the form of spiritual liberation. The spiritual life, in this regard, is not man in his experience of finitude questing for infinitude, but man realizing his infinitude in the act of accepting his finitude. The very intimation of something greater than ourselves is our awareness of ourselves as the Infinite manifesting itself as the finite.

To accept one's finitude is to delve into the heart of individuality, and it is here that spirituality and psychology meet. So much has been written in the area of psychology and religion that one can easily get lost in its expansive body of terms, concepts, theories, and analogical models. In the spirit of William of Occam we seek the elegance of simplicity, to penetrate to the heart of the matter. We fear that if we do not discuss religious or spiritual ideas in supernatural terms, they will necessarily be reduced to naturalistic terms, and we will become pantheists. The general purview of spirituality must include such things as angels and spirits of the dead, afterlife and reincarnation, visions and premonitions, and doctrines and rituals. Any suggestion of affinity between the spiritual and the natural or everyday worlds is a threat to the tenability of spirituality because spirit and nature are considered opposites. Seen as such, any attempt to demystify or bring "down to earth" the spiritual element would seem to despiritualize it. If spirit and nature are not posited as opposites, as mutually exclusive – that is, if we acknowledge the *nonduality* that transcends them - we are less susceptible to the needless confusion arising from distinctions that are principally artifacts of the inherent dualism of language and thought. To suggest that the spiritual life lies in the acceptance of finitude or individuality, that the spiritual need not be polarized from the everyday or mundane, only reduces the spiritual to the natural if the two are opposed.

If the Infinite ultimately transcends all dualisms while also embracing them, to speak of the spiritual in mundane terms is not to reduce the spiritual but to ennoble the mundane. The spiritual can only be reduced to the natural if the natural is already reduced, which is the inevitable result of creating this schism in the first place. Reductionism strikes hard when the natural or mundane is devalued as "just" this or "simply" that, ignoring that as a manifestation of the Infinite, the inherent nature of finitude could never be spiritually bereft. Awed by the very fact of existence, the young child and the spiritually aware adult can appreciate the profundity of a sunset or budding flower without invoking exclusively religious or spiritual constructs. Spirit and nature are not split asunder, and the divine is not hopelessly sought in another place and time, as if the manifest universe were no more than some insipid epiphenomenon.

Permeating psychological, anthropological, and biophysical thought is the rudimentary assumption that man is essentially alone, a sentient mass of flesh in an otherwise cold and mechanistic universe, and a creature of consciousness encapsulated in his own skull. This principle and experience of existential alienation engenders profound terror, for in our experience of ourselves as fragmented or splintered from the greater whole we become inconsequential, and our lives are seen to have no real meaning. Our existence is no more significant than had we never existed at all. There are many who believe that we should accept this principle and experience axiomatically, for any thought to the contrary is merely an attempt to escape the inescapable reality of our ultimate aloneness (Heidegger 1927; Husserl 1913; Kierkegaard 1846; Sartre 1943). Others view this experience as illusory, and view thought to the contrary not as escapism, but as a movement to render the illusion transparent (Suzuki 1949, 1956; Watts 1948, 1957).

The dawning of ego consciousness is a normal developmental phase in the evolution of individual consciousness. In the earlier stages of ontogenesis the wondrous object world is the wholly predominant reality. There are only vague intimations of the reality of the knowing Subject or conscious Self, for it is completely lost or absorbed in the experience of the object. The experience of subjectivity is introduced with the consciousness of ego. As ontogenesis proceeds there are developments in cognitive, psychosocial, and biological functioning that draw a considerable amount of conscious attention to the psychophysical organism. Physical changes and surging hormones throw the biological organism into stark relief. As language enters into social discourse the individual becomes a social object with a reflected concept of herself, typically constituted by the adjectives and labels that are assigned to her. With the increasing capacity to grasp higher-order categorical abstractions, further attention is drawn to one's self-concept and identity as it is intricately woven into the fabric of social nomenclature and meaning. While navigating the world of adult human interaction and its politics, considerable attention must be focused on one's persona or social face, and on the act of impression management necessary for this presentation of self. With this massive attentional consumption by the ego or psychophysical organism, there are still only vague intimations of the knowing Subject or conscious Self, for it is lost in the ego experience, which is a particular aspect of the general object experience. It is this state of mind that we refer to as ego consciousness, and true subjectivity is still a nonexperience. Yet since the ego experience is more proximal, compelling, and vivid than the remainder of the object field, it is designated and experienced as *oneself*, the true identity, or the subject of all that is known and experienced.

Disconcerting only because of its unfamiliarity, a moment's reflection reveals that the ego or psychophysical organism is actually not the subject of experience, but a circumscribed, more central and proximal portion of the object field in which the conscious Self gets lost or absorbed. The phenomenology of the psychophysical organism, the thoughts, feelings, perceptions, sensations, memories, and anticipations, are all objects of knowledge; the truly subjective side of experience defies description, and is the cornerstone of religion, spirituality, mysticism, and metaphysics. The knowing Subject, or conscious Self, in other words, is a transcendent entity, but no less "oneself" because of its transcendence. In fact, it is *the* Self, the foundation of knowledge and reality, the very ground of being.

To speak of ego consciousness as a developmental phase in the evolution of consciousness implies the ultimate "awakening" of the Self to its own nature, as distinct, though inseparable, from the field of ego and non-ego object experience. If the Self is "oneself" ultimately, its transcendence renders any attempt to distinguish the psychological from the spiritual as theoretically inelegant and redundant. It is a grave error and misunderstanding of Eastern philosophies to suggest that the ego or psychophysical organism is in some way an unreality or illusion. It is nihilism that takes the ego experience, and the general object experience, and invalidates them ontologically. The illusion is the experience that the psychophysical organism is the center of being, or ultimately "oneself," and this illusion is created when the knowing Subject or conscious Self is absorbed in, or identified with, the ego experience. When reference is made to the "ego illusion," this is not to say that the illusion is the ego itself, but rather the experience of being ontologically limited and bound by it. To render the ego illusion transparent is not to negate the ego, but to know it as an object of knowledge like all objects of knowledge, as distinct from the knowing Subject or conscious Self. Conscious of itself, the Self continues to know the object world but no longer identifies with it, and in this awakening it realizes its essential transcendence and infinitude. The illusory nature of ego consciousness and the impression of aloneness are revealed, and any foundation for the meaninglessness and futility of existential anxiety is undermined.

To say that the awakened Self consciously knows the world of finite objects is to say that it loves those objects for their very finitude. The movement of the transcendent Self or Spirit is to delve into the heart of individuality, and in this movement is found spiritual liberation and the spiritual life. We shall see that the answer to the problem of existential alienation and spiritual impoverishment is the process of individuation, or the articulation and development of personality, for in this mundane movement of human psychology is the perfect exemplification of the formative *Logos*, or the Infinite Spirit manifesting itself in finite form.

II
Spirit and Form

We begin with the reality of everyday life, the world of finite objects, or the world that is known and can be known. If words are to do it any justice, only indefinite variability and unceasing movement can even begin to approximate its richness. It is a world of colors and shapes, textures and sounds, feelings and ideas. It ranges aesthetically from exquisite beauty to horrific ugliness, and is forever in a state of flux.

Among their myriad qualities, finite objects of knowledge may be distal or proximal. The mountains on the horizon, for example, are clearly farther away than the chair in which I am sitting, whereas the sensations in my body and the thoughts in my head are clearly nearer. Yet when we speak of distal and proximal we must have a point of reference, for these are strictly relative concepts. We must ask, "Distal and proximal in relation to what?" The answer will be, "in relation to me, of course," but we must be more specific. If by *me* I mean my physical body, I can certainly say that the mountains are distant and the chair is near. But it must be remembered that my body, either as internal sensations or as a visual percept, is also a finite object of knowledge that is near - nearer, in fact, than the chair. What, then, is the *me* in relation to which distal and proximal make sense? I can say that perhaps it is my very thoughts and feelings, and again I must be reminded that thoughts and feelings are finite objects of knowledge as well. They are strikingly nearer than the mountains, but remain finite objects. It seems that in my attempt to define myself I consistently discern known objects. What, then, is the *me* that stands in relation to these objects, that knows these objects?

We may approach the question from a different angle. That which is finite is, by definition, a contingency or determination. Finite objects cannot be self-determining and self-sustaining, but must, by virtue of their finitude, refer to and depend upon something else for their existence. Finite objects, in other words, must be grounded in something greater than themselves, lest we are forced to grapple with the absurdity of something arising from nothing. We may say, then, that finite existence is grounded in *infinite being*.

Moreover, in considering the nature of finite existence we discover the inextricable relationship between knowledge and reality. Whereas it would be egocentric presumption to assert that what we do not know does not exist, simple introspection reveals that what we do know we know only in a field of consciousness. From the standpoint of human experience, *finite existence is that which is known*, for where there is no knowledge or consciousness there is no reality.

If finite existence is that which is known, it must stand in relation to *that which knows*. The necessity of this relationship is not simply one of grammar and logic. Finite objects of knowledge, for their very epistemological status as things known, imply the presence of a knowing subject. Finite objects stand in relation to one another, and these relations articulate their respective, relative qualities. But finite objects also stand in relation to that which knows for their absolute quality, or very fact of being, and are thus said to be grounded in it.

If finite existence or known objects must be grounded in infinite being, in one respect, or a knowing subject, in another, may we not say that the two are one and the same, and that as finite existence is that which is known, *infinite being is that which knows*? To speak of infinite being as a knowing subject, or as conscious, should not be unfamiliar since traditional religious thinking represents God the Infinite as not only omnipotent but as omniscient as well.

The knowing subject, or the conscious Self, is that "central point of being upon which our knowledge of existence depends" (Watts 1948, 76). It is the *here* in relation to which all objects of knowledge are relatively distal or proximal. As a particular viewpoint, the conscious Self knows a world of finite objects, of things and events. These objects, again, may be far or near, or they may be so near that, mistakenly, they are no longer considered objective experiences because they are internal. Our thoughts, for example, or our feelings or memories, are *objective experiences within us*. That they are internal does not make them subjective. Although they are discerned by introspection, they are still finite objects in the sense that they are things known, not to be confused with that which knows. We intuit this very principle when we say "I have an idea," as opposed to "I *am* an idea." The conscious Self, in other words, distinguishes itself from everything that it knows, or that can be known.

As the knower, the Self cannot know itself objectively, or as an object. This would be like expecting someone to turn around quickly and catch a glimpse of himself. However, the Self does not need to know itself objectively, any more than light, which is naturally luminous, needs to illuminate itself. The knowing subject knows the finite world objectively, whereas it knows itself subjectively or immediately. Although this latter kind of knowledge is not amenable to the objectivism of scientific reason, a little introspection will reveal how profoundly certain and self-evident it is, more than anything that can be derived from logical positivism (Watts 1948).

It becomes apparent that the knowing subject or conscious Self is a finite consciousness in that it is limited in scope. It corresponds to the particular awareness of any given individual. Yet if infinite being is that which knows, or the subject of knowledge, how can its consciousness be finite? We can approach this question by looking to the seat or foundation of finite consciousness. It is here that we can fall into the traps set by epiphenomenalism and nihilism, or be forced to draw a more profound conclusion.

Epiphenomenalism argues that consciousness is some sort of fluke, or an incidental by-product of neurochemical activity, and that in and of itself is of no consequence and has no true reality. The physical world of neurochemical activity is real, and thus a phenomenon, whereas the world of human consciousness is but an *epi*phenomenon, ultimately not worth consideration. The absurdity of this notion is that it conveniently precludes itself from its own rule. Since the theory of epiphenomenalism is itself a product of human consciousness, then it too must be an epiphenomenon, not to be considered as having any consequence. In every reductionistic philosophy we must inevitably reduce the reduction itself.

If finite consciousness has its own reality, we must still look to its foundation, since anything that is finite cannot be groundless. It would be a greater absurdity than epiphenomenalism to suggest that finite consciousness arises ex nihilo. The very idea of something from nothing is actually a pseudo-idea that comes from playing with words and concepts. It suggests that the most infinite depths of being are less than what is manifested, and not more. This renders the universe meaningless, since it is grounded in an empty void. As with all nihilistic and reductionstic philosophies, if the universe is ultimately meaningless, so is the philosophy itself.

If not a contingent artifact of the organic or physical world, and if not the absurdity of something arising from nothing, finite consciousness, which cannot be groundless, must then be seen as grounded in, or a manifestation of, infinite consciousness. Again, conceiving of infinite consciousness, or that the Infinite is conscious, should not be difficult since we already think of God as the All Knowing. If infinite being is that which knows, it must also be infinite in its consciousness. Infinite being or consciousness is the foundation of the universe. Whereas it can never be an object of knowledge, for there is no position outside or away from it from which to view it objectively, it is the foundation of knowledge and reality. It is the Absolute Ground of Being.

Now it may seem strange to describe consciousness as the foundation or ground of anything, since consciousness is ephemeral and not palpable. We like to think of foundations as solid, as in the solid base of a physical structure or a solid education. Solidity implies substance and palpability, literally or figuratively something we can stand on or wrap our hands around. But consciousness is impalpable. It is sizeless, since it does not occupy space. It is essentially without content or form, while being the basis for content and form. It cannot be grasped, physically or conceptually. How then can anything be grounded in it?

From a completely different perspective we draw the same conclusions about the ground of being. Trusting the validity of that which is known subjectively through introspection has, in the modern world, been a bit of a problem. We learn to be empiricists, to trust only that which can be seen, touched, or otherwise measured. The ultimate expression of logical positivism is the study of the physical world. The gurus of quantum physics start with what is macroscopically experienced as solid substance, or matter, and then develop the equipment and techniques to penetrate the depths of this substance by studying it subatomically. As they go "smaller and smaller," trying to get closer to the foundation, they discover that it becomes more elusive. They develop the concept of a quantum field that underlies all manifest subatomic phenomena and without which they would have no existence. This field is not to be reified, but conceived as pure process. They discover that how the field manifests itself is a function of how they measure it. If they attempt to study motion, it appears as waves.

If they attempt to study position, it appears as particles. The point is that the observed cannot be separated from the observer, and therefore we can never have a truly objective view of the field. It cannot be made an object of knowledge, and, in objective terms, can only be known analogically as it is created in the process of measurement. In much the same way, different prisms will refract or "represent" light differently. Moreover, we are told that waves are not actual but probable, and that the particles do not actually exist but show tendencies to exist. This is the description par excellence of the impalpable and ephemeral, and it is the description of the foundation of the physical universe (Capra 1975). Far less like material *stuff* and more like pure spirit, the quantum field descriptively sounds much like the infinite consciousness of God.

From the standpoint of atomic and subatomic physics there is an implied distinction between spirit and form. The quantum field, in its intractable elusiveness, most closely fits the definition of pure spirit. The motion or activity of this field, or what it does, is the foundation for the phenomenology of color, shape, and sound. In other words, the particles and waves generated by the field, and their interactions in the form of reflected light or compressions and rarefactions of air translating into the neurochemical activity of eye, ear, and brain, "result" in consciousness as the awareness of form. The physicists will tell us that "outside" our consciousness there is no shape or color or sound, but rather whirling dances of electricity, varying wavelengths of light, and physical disturbances in the air. Yet are these not also illustrations of form in the sense that they are forms of motion of the field? And how are they out of our consciousness if they are conscious ideas or the conscious registration of experimental information in the mind of the scientist? The very idea of externality or outside consciousness is a conscious idea, something that is in, or an object of, our consciousness. No matter how hard we try, we cannot step out of our consciousness, and this is not an argument for solipsism. Space and time, being finite objects of knowledge, are also aspects of consciousness, and therefore it makes no difference to say that things and events occur in a field of consciousness, or that they occur in a space-time continuum (Watts 1948). The quantum field as it is known, either in the form of a child contemplating a bright flower or a scientist studying the subatomic universe, is form. The quantum field as it *knows* is the objectively unknowable spirit. We may say, then, that *spirit creates form in the act of knowing it.*

11

In finite terms it can be said that infinite consciousness knows every aspect of the entire finite order simultaneously, and as immediately present to its entire self. It must know everything simultaneously since it transcends the finite time series of knowing things successively. It must know things as immediately present since nothing can be away from the Infinite to be known at a distance. And it must know things with its entire self since the Infinite remains undivided. From a finite standpoint, such omniscience is necessarily incomprehensible (Watts 1948).

Yet there is a finite standpoint. Infinite consciousness, by virtue of its infinitude, has the freedom and ability to restrict itself by adopting finite points of view. Each point of view corresponds to the particular awareness of any given individual. Finite consciousness, or the knowing subject or Self, is thus a mode of infinite consciousness, and in essence of the same substance. It is thus that the consciousness of man, not that which this consciousness knows, is identical to the Infinite Consciousness, or the consciousness of God. Since the Infinite, while adopting finite points of view, never loses its infinitude, it makes no difference to say that there is an indefinite number of conscious selves, or that there is but one Self simultaneously adopting an indefinite number of perspectives (Watts 1948).

We come to the same realization when we consider that the religious mind relates to God as the Great Other, as up or out there, or deep within, but ontologically distinct from man, and a potential object of his knowledge. The insistence upon ontological distinction is of paramount importance, for the very idea of a common ground or identity between man and God where the polarity of man and God is transcended constitutes the most profound heresy, and the ultimate taboo. The polarity of man as subject and God as object must be maintained, ultimately leaving man utterly alone in his feeling of absolute separateness from God.

The problem with God as the Great Other is that God can never be made an object of knowledge. Only finite things can be objects of knowledge, and God, by definition, is infinite. The Infinite can never be made an object of knowledge because there is no position or viewpoint away from the Infinite from which it can be viewed objectively. Religion recognizes the ineffability of God as an object and admonishes us not to be deceived by images of him, graven or otherwise. Yet experientially we continue to seek affinity with him, which is clearly a subject relating to an object.

If we shift from a consideration of God as object to God as subject, we encounter profound implications. To suggest, in other words, that God is not, and could never be, an object of human knowledge, but is instead the subject of knowledge, or that within us which knows, is to suggest that our very consciousness is of one substance with the consciousness of God.

The notion of a common ground or identity between man and God typically invokes accusations of heresy. Yet there is profound misunderstanding on this issue, principally because of the confusion of man as the knowing subject with man as the known object. Man as the known or designated individual is not *that which knows*. Rather, it is his thoughts, sensations, feelings, memories, anticipations, values, and personality, all of which are things known and to be distinguished from that which knows. To speak of an identity between man and God is thus not to say that man *as man* is God, but that the consciousness or basic awareness of man is a mode of expression of the consciousness of God. When the reality of this common ground is not simply the premise of intellectual argument but an intimate fact of experience, the need to seek affinity with God disappears, since there is no longer the experience of a gulf or discontinuity between God and the center of our being.

Where infinite consciousness knows itself as the ultimate subject and ground of knowledge and being, or, in religious terms, when the immediate and inescapable presence of God is the most self-evident fact of experience, there is no internal spiritual impoverishment pressing us to seek completion from something outside ourselves. We continue to need our loving relationships and our labors of love, but being spiritually replete, there is no need to take from life anxiously and greedily, or to be paranoid and contemptuous. Instead, the natural inclination is to give to the world through an act of self-abandonment or selfless love. It becomes apparent that it is only when we are ordered thus to our proper center that we can truly give of ourselves.

III
Liberating the Spirit

Self-abandonment or selfless love is the total acceptance of things as they are. It is the love of finite things, loving them for their very finitude and limitations. This acceptance is not a philosophy of passive acquiescence, or an excuse for inertness and lack of movement or growth. On the contrary, to love something for its finitude is not simply to sit and look at it, but to develop it in accordance with its limitations. Since the features that limit an object and make it finite also define it and give it its uniqueness, to develop something in accordance with its limitations is thus to cultivate its individuality. This love is *self*less because there is no confusion of oneself with the finite object. The finite object, in other words, is developed in accordance with *its* limitations, and not one's idea of what it should be, and these are limitations not in the sense of restriction or impoverishment but in the sense of definition and individuality. Within this framework of delineated individuality, the potential for growth and development is limitless. This process of liberation through definition is the paradox of discovering freedom within structure.

Freedom, as a construct and an experience, is the premier human consideration and objective. Without it, life is ultimately meaningless. On the most concrete level we speak of freedom from the physical bondage of slavery and indentured servitude. With these basics, we further espouse freedom of thought, speech, and expression, and the freedom to pursue happiness. Yet even within the social configurations of democracy and free enterprise freedom is uncommon, and we know this because happiness is uncommon. Without a true understanding and experience of its nature, freedom is easily reduced to its own caricature of libertarianism and contrived or exaggerated individuality. The essential freedom, and the key to happiness, is founded upon the liberated spirit, and such liberation inheres in, and derives from, the act of cultivating individuality of form. Secular culture appears not to provide an institutionalized vehicle for such liberation, so we must turn our attention to organized religion.

The practice of religion is a double-edged sword. One is either a fanatic or a hypocrite. The fanatic lives by the letter of the law. He is a literalist, a concrete thinker, and ultimately a fascist. His position must be defended at all costs, even if it pushes him to acts of cruelty or barbarism. His inflexibility is absolute, and at most he will tolerate intelligent and articulate viewpoints that differ from his own as interesting but misguided.

The hypocrite lives by the "spirit" of the law, which, by definition, leaves considerable room for interpretation. He picks and chooses, selecting the holidays to be observed, which traditions to follow, and what he does and does not believe. The hypocrisy is that his religion is tailored to his personal needs and agenda, incorporating what "works" in his life, and dismissing what is inconvenient. All of this is completely rationalized.

Yet there are other hypocrisies that afflict hypocrite and fanatic alike. Most prominent is a disparity between one's personal and social definition of self as a "religious" being, and a corresponding character structure that is conspicuously deficient. One can be mired in tradition, dogma, and moral judgment and still be an awful person. This disparity cannot be overlooked, lest we truly settle for a philosophy of *do as I say, not as I do.* It might be hoped that a true spiritual consciousness would have more of a unitive than a separative effect on personality and social relations.

Perhaps the most profound hypocrisy, more specifically stated, is a lack of congruence between the outward motions and the internal experience of a religious person. One may read and study scripture, attend services, participate in ceremony and ritual, and all the while remain spiritually bereft. It is a fascinating phenomenon, and one worthy of consideration.

Some practice their religion because it is expected of them. It is the thing to do. There may or may not be an element of commitment and emotional intensity, but religious practice and belief is foisted on them. They do not come to it. This, in itself, is spiritual death, as the potential for freedom is clipped from the beginning.

Others have taken the opportunity to step back, examine their beliefs, and then embrace them nonetheless. In these instances we find an even greater intensity of commitment and emotional involvement. Yet when examining an individual's consciousness in terms of how spiritually conscious or aware he truly is, we must revert to the issue of character. The unattractive fact is that increasing orthodoxy brings increasing susceptibility to tribalism, which is contempt for others, and, in the extreme, the very renunciation of the secular and even physical world. The irony is that this posture of condescension and spiritual one-upmanship is as antireligious as can be, and shows a complete misunderstanding of the idea of God as the Infinite. For if God is infinite, there is no position or viewpoint outside or away from God such that one person or group can be closer to him than another.

The most blatant and crudest form of incongruence between outward motion and internal experience is the gesturing in religious contexts of those who wish to appear righteous and observant, but who secretly and implicitly collude to sustain nothing more than a social venue for displaying the latest fashions and fulfilling a need for gossip and social comparison. Holidays are celebrated because it is the thing to do, and typically the core meaning and experience are diluted or totally obscured by the more peripheral, cultural features of the holidays, plus the manipulations of the media.

The analysis of congruence between motion and experience underscores how little emphasis is typically placed on the subjective experience or phenomenology of the individual. Getting lost in the outward trappings of religious behavior without congruent subjective experience is the hypocrisy of form without content. No matter how elegant the masonry and trimmings of an architectural structure, a flimsy or decaying infrastructure renders it ultimately worthless. A consciousness dictated by fanatical intolerance, pragmatic motives, automation, contempt and isolationism, or the need for impression management can hardly be considered spiritual without making a mockery of the term. If this is the consciousness that accompanies religious behavior, we must then confront the existential nightmare of lifeless action, or rote, repetitive behavior overlying a smothered spirit and diseased soul. Unless we are willing to forfeit the capacity for happiness, this situation simply will not do.

If neither religious nor secular configurations provide an institutional venue for a true liberation of the spirit, are we left with no alternative but despair? Surely there must be people who are truly happy and fulfilled. There must be those who take delight in their work and relationships, who constantly evolve and help others evolve in the process. They are those who ride the wings of an indomitable life force and presence, yet without the bombastic preaching of the moralists and their incessant talk of God and religion. If we surrender to the barrenness of abject cynicism and disallow the possibility of such people, we are left with nothing but the choice between a preordained life of unhappiness and suicide. Despair is the equivalent of spiritual and psychological death, and there is thus a measure of fortitude involved in facing and accepting the boundless possibilities of life. If we allow for the possibility of those who enjoy spiritual liberation, it is inevitable that we ask by what means or act of grace they are blessed with this invaluable gift.

Selfless love compels us to give ourselves to others and to life, and it is selfless because it is based on a clear distinction between oneself and the object. The object is object qua object, the thing in itself, with its particular limitations and finitude recognized and accepted. Moreover, this acceptance is not simply a mental attitude but an act, and is therefore not passive or acquiescent. It is the act of cultivating individuality, or developing the finite object in accordance with its limitations, definition, and uniqueness. This act of cultivation or selfless love is the liberated spirit, and only through it can one discover true freedom and happiness.

The act of cultivating or perfecting form is the basis of all art and science; it matters not whether we are clipping a bonsai tree in a manner that dignifies it, or articulating a theory on the basis of ongoing research. Both tree and theory are forms in the sense that they are finite objects of knowledge. To delineate and cultivate individuality of form is to liberate the spirit in the form, and is, at the same time, an act of the liberated spirit. It is an outpouring of love so that the finite object can enjoy the same freedom, the same opportunity for the outward volution of its most central and inherent properties, which is the principle of organic life.

Perhaps, then, there is indeed an institutional secular venue for the liberation of the spirit. As the profound is often discovered in the obvious, perhaps it is the simple institution of parenthood. Indeed, the illustration par excellence of selfless love is the act of artful child rearing, for children, too, are forms, and from the human standpoint, our most precious ones. We can illustrate the principle of artful child rearing by distinguishing between the ideal childhood and the typical childhood.

The Ideal Childhood

A child with a unique genetic configuration is born to a world of people, things, and events. Far from being a blank slate, the child already has particular temperamental characteristics, undiscovered talents and aptitudes, and the potential for certain interests and personality traits (Eaves, Eysenck, and Martin 1989; Eysenck 1967; Plomin and McClearn 1993; Thomas and Chess 1977). Immediately and simultaneously, child and world react to each other. As the world affects the child, so it is affected by the child. An infant is stirred by its mother's irritability, yet some of this irritability may be a response to an inconsolable infant. What becomes apparent is that the actions of the child and of the world are inextricable, and cannot be unraveled in any meaningful way. The popular question of whether personality is a matter of nature or nurture or, if both, in what proportion, is then seen to be theoretically immature and of no practical value. The real question is how the nurturing process can work with the unique configuration of the child toward the cultivation of individuality.

The principle of *working with* refers to a way of relating to the world that respects the fundamental nature of things. An architect, for example, might design a home to adapt to the irregularities of hilly terrain, rather than leveling the land first. A sailor cannot change the wind, but instead uses it by adjusting his sails. The ideal childhood, in this regard, is one in which parents and teachers respect the fundamental nature of the child, and work with it to facilitate its development. Parenting and teaching as such are the most important of the interpersonal arts, and their success rests upon the application of three profoundly simple principles: *clear mirroring, free exploration*, and *emotional security*.

Clear mirroring is the act of discerning the particular talents and aptitudes of a child, and then reflecting them by pointing them out to the child. In this way, the child is made aware of that which defines and distinguishes her ("I'm smart in math," "I'm a good artist"), and her self-esteem is enriched through knowing and appreciating her strengths.

Free exploration is the opportunity for *divergent experience*: to think and feel expansively, and thereby come to one's own interests and ideas. Through this process the awareness of oneself is further articulated, and one's self-esteem is further enriched by the implied faith of those who allow for this freedom.

Emotional security is the ongoing experience of feeling loved and protected. As the initial and ultimate foundation of self-esteem, it facilitates clear mirroring by enabling the child to believe the positive evaluations of others. As the basis for feeling safe in the world, it provides the confidence needed for free exploration.

The ideal outcome of the ideal childhood is twofold. First, because of the loving and respectful relationships that laid the path for the child's good feeling and clarity of self, she will be able to form loving and respectful relationships. Second, because she is clear about her true talents and interests, she will be able to reconcile them by pursuing that which she both enjoys and does well, ultimately fashioning a career path wherein the line between work and play is forever blurred. Feeling personally and professionally fulfilled in her relationships and work, experiencing the joy of ongoing growth and self-discovery while helping others do the same, such an individual exemplifies the personality of the liberated spirit. Her particular theism, or whether she is theistic at all, is irrelevant to her freedom. What matters is the richness and purity of her subjective life, and the consequent outpouring of love that touches the minds and hearts of those who come in contact with her.

The Typical Childhood

In the typical childhood the cultivation of the individuality of the child is not the premier consideration of the parent. This can be for a variety of reasons, and its effects can vary in degree and form. The act of parenting, in this regard, works against the nature of the child by failing to apply the principles of clear mirroring, free exploration, and emotional security. This can best be understood by considering these principles in their inverted forms.

The inverse of clear mirroring is *distorted mirroring*. Distorted mirroring is when parents lead children to believe that they have talents and aptitudes that they do not, or that they do not have aptitudes and talents that they do. For example, one may be a frustrated musician who wishes to see musical brilliance in her child when it simply is not there. Or a parent may be intellectually insecure and perhaps need to make her formidably bright child feel stupid. The net effect is that the child is left with a distorted self-image, not unlike the misrepresentative reflections from an amusement park mirror.

The inverse of free exploration is *intellectual and emotional constriction*. Here there is no divergence of experience, as children are denied the opportunity to come to their own interests and ideas. Actual or potential interests are squashed when the child is forced to pursue activities and career paths that have no personal meaning and are significant only to the parent. This culminates in the tragedy of *false ambition*. Intellectual freedom is prohibited when ideas, attitudes, and beliefs are imposed on the child, or presented with the imperative that they not be questioned. The very act of thinking is clipped, and there is never a completed process of questioning ideas first, and then accepting, rejecting, or modifying them. In effect, the mind of the child is removed from the equation, and with little wonder, the "difficult-to-manage" child is described as "having a mind of her own."

The inverse of emotional security is *fearful clinging*. Having never felt consistently loved, the child feels inferior, and this feeling of inferiority endures because any praise or recognition received outside the home or later in life is inevitably met with skepticism ("How can anybody know me better than my own parents?"). Having never felt held and protected, the child feels insecure and fearful of the world. Lacking the confidence for exploration and discovery of the world and herself, her alternative is to seek security in self-limitation by anxiously clinging to the known and familiar.

The typical outcome of the typical childhood is that, to varying degrees and in varying forms, the child does not know who she truly is, and, as a result, does not and cannot operate from a true center of being. Proceeding from the periphery, from a position of existential inauthenticity, she never truly burgeons because her spirit is obstructed from expression. Yet despite the obscuring presence of false reflections and other people's ideas, interests, and aspirations, the true form lies within, in both its actual and potential aspects.

No childhood is ideal in the sense of a total absence of pain, loss, frustration, and heartbreak. Yet artful child rearing is real, not simply an abstraction or reification. It must be ascribed ontological validity because it is of consequence. This is by no means to suggest even the possibility of a perfect correlation between artful child rearing and the ideal outcome. It is possible for this rearing to fail, as it is possible for the ideal outcome to arise in the absence of this rearing. But this does not diminish the power of the human act, or the impact of a family matrix that offers love *and* freedom. Even if we are but specks of dust in an inestimably large universe, do we contain any less potential power than the unsplit atoms that are but specks to us? In a universe of uncertainty we retain the ability to influence the likelihood of outcomes or events, such as raising an emotionally healthy child who knows who she is and is thus able to operate from a true center of being.

Whether it arises by artful means or grace, spiritual liberation is certainly not the norm. Throughout childhood the spirit is typically obstructed from expression, and this state of disorder, like any other, implies the possibility of a cure. We are compelled, then, to discern, along with artful child rearing, a second, remedial secular venue for the liberation of the spirit. Otherwise, we remain forever wandering in darkness.

IV
Central and Peripheral Being

In the history of an intellectual culture, terms and concepts come into vogue. Like great songs that are overplayed, that they can grow tiresome does not diminish their intrinsic value. New ideas may be beneficently adopted from their original contexts, or they may be snatched and prostituted for personal gain. Again, their intrinsic value remains unaffected. The West Coast of the United States in the 1960s and 70s, for example, was the mecca for a spiritual and sociopolitical revolution that assimilated, and was fueled by, ideological and philosophical influences of Asian culture. The schools of psychology and the religious and political bodies of the United States and Europe were progressively juxtaposed to, and assimilated, the ways of the East. Hinduism, Taoism, and Buddhism, particularly Zen, flourished in their new venues, and were disseminated widely and quickly. What was lacking in our own ways created a hunger and readiness for compensation and balance, and we forged new approaches to old systems of politics, religion, medicine, and psychotherapy. There were those who were quite serious about this revolution, and thus congruent in their experience. Others were, to varying degrees, traditionalists, but congruent still. And then there were the truly incongruous souls who approached the movement with insincerity, working, in effect, to create an image, to fit in, to be cool. It was the last who were principally responsible for many critical terms and concepts becoming clichéd, hence to be mockingly equated with California, and ultimately to be capped with "finger quotations" whenever mentioned. Minds were not to be expanded, new doors of perception were not to be opened, and experiences were not to be shared without the contemptuous smirks of insecure pseudointellectuals boosting themselves through the denigration of invaluable ideas.

One of those "sixties" terms and concepts that must be reintroduced is that of being *centered*, or operating from a *center of being*. In the most vividly physical sense, this experience can be appreciated in the various practices of sitting meditation. Through deep breathing and keen physiological awareness we somatically locate our center of gravity in the abdominal region of the body. We know that this centering is a legitimate phenomenon and not simply a reification because, when maintained, it becomes exceedingly difficult for us to be knocked off balance when assuming the more active standing postures such as tai chi and the martial arts. With deep breathing the body becomes relaxed, and the mind stilled and quieted. We think of this state as the psychological sense of being centered. It would be a mistake, however, to assume that a stilled and quieted mind is an empty mind. To the contrary, it is quite alert and can be replete with content. Like an undisturbed lake reflecting geese flying overhead, it entertains thoughts, feelings, and sense-impressions without rejecting them or becoming affixed to them. Sensory experience, feelings, and emotions rise and fall continually, never rejected and never hypnotically consumptive of attention. Trains of thought are calmly watched and not blindly boarded. Thus, we are not carried away by them, losing our awareness of the moment in which they occur. Awareness of the moment and of the things and events in it is the Infinite Consciousness assuming a finite point of view, knowing itself immediately and subjectively as such, and as the source and ground of all that is objectively known. It consciously knows or loves the finite object in the act of self-abandonment, and does not lose itself in it through unconscious identification. However, since infinite consciousness, while adopting finite points of view, never loses its essential infinitude, from a broader standpoint we may say that the knowing subject, *even when most absorbed in the things known*, is always or eternally still, quiet and centered. Like the reflecting lake, it readily surrenders itself to the finite world. Yet the fact of its essential infinitude and transcendent purity means that while it is never separate from finite reality, it can never be touched by it either.

The conscious Self or knowing subject is the deliberate self-limitation of the Infinite Consciousness as it assumes finite or particular points of view. Each viewpoint corresponds to the particular awareness of any given individual, which is essentially a specific field of consciousness with oneself as the central node or point of being. The conscious Self knows a world of finite objects, of things and events. Central and proximal to the Self in this field of consciousness is the empirical ego, or the known and designated individual. This is man as the known object, as a psychic life of thoughts, sensations, feelings, memories, anticipations, and values. It is the individual as known to himself and others, as a particular character, personality, and set of constitutional attributes, and as an expansive mosaic of identificatory roles, labels, and numbers that define and position him in the larger social structure. All of the aforementioned are finite objects in that they are things known, to be distinguished from that which knows. Man as the known object, in other words, must stand in relation to man as the knowing subject. Man as the knowing subject or conscious Self is thus the interior knower of himself as the known object. The conscious Self cannot be the object of its own knowledge because it is distinguishable from all that it knows and can be known. Although finite or limited in scope, as a self-limitation of infinite consciousness it is of one substance with infinite consciousness, and is itself not a finite object, but that which knows and thus transcends finite objects.

The Infinite Consciousness assumes a finite point of view, and either knows itself as such and consciously knows the world of finite objects, or loses itself through unconscious identification with the world of finite objects. In the biographically early stages of individual consciousness the Self is unconsciously and indiscriminately identified with the entire field of known objects, so there is little or no awareness of self or of the subjective side of knowledge. With ontogenetic development and increasing discriminatory capacity the Self no longer identifies with the entire field of known objects, but only with the empirical ego. The empirical ego is thus experienced as the knowing subject, with the remainder of the field now disidentified with the Self and clearly experienced as the known object. When, as rarely happens, the Self awakens to its true nature as transcendent and distinct from the empirical ego as well - when it consciously knows the empirical ego as a finite object - it realizes its own essential infinitude.

In its infinitude the Self is replete, and therefore its nature is to give or abandon itself to the finite order, which includes the empirical ego. The conscious Self knows the finite object by accepting its limitations, or that which defines it. In this act of knowing the Self abandons itself, or gives itself up, to the finite object, as the eye gives itself up to what it sees, or the mind to its thoughts. In this profound and fundamental sense it is the principle of love that brings the finite order into being. When the act of love or self-abandonment is unconscious, the Self is identified with the ego.

Because of the ego's finitude the Self experiences itself as such, as a finite object, and is thus introduced to the anxiety of isolation and insecurity. In its quest to allay this dread the Self, as identified with the ego, becomes acquisitive; it takes or appropriates unto itself to bolster itself and dispel the anguish of tentativeness. In short, its action becomes separative. When the act of love is conscious, the Self knows its distinct and proper nature, and thus its essential infinity. Insecure not and fearing not, it is the cup that runneth over, for in its utter repletion its only mode of action is to give, to be unitive.

The conscious Self is eternally abandoning or giving itself to the finite world in an act of accepting or loving its limitations. It is in this act that the finite world is known and created. When the act of abandonment is unconscious and the Self is lost in the ego, the separative movement, with its implicit insecurity, looks to possess form, to control, subjugate, or otherwise violate its nature. When the act of abandonment is conscious, the unitive movement of the Self looks not to possess form, but to cultivate it, or develop it in accordance with its limitations. By not confusing the finite object with oneself the love is *selfless*, and one is thus detached in the true Hindu and Buddhist sense. To cultivate individuality of form is to articulate or define it *as it is*, actually and potentially, and thus allow for its growth and development as such. Within the framework of the object's delineated individuality is the opportunity for the outward volution of its most central and inherent properties, which is the principle of life. This paradox of freedom within structure is the liberation of the spirit in the form.

One is centered when the conscious Self knows itself immediately and subjectively as the deliberate self-limitation of the Infinite Consciousness, and as the foundation of all knowledge and reality. Operating from a center of being involves the unfolding of form as it is clearly and accurately defined. It is form turning itself inside out, as it were, such that the properties manifesting later in the time series are progressively of a more central and integral nature. It is an act of constant burgeoning. It is liberation and spiritual freedom in the truest sense, and the monolithic answer to the meaning of happiness. In the absence of clear definition, shrouded in ambiguity from the nonacceptance of neglect or selfish love, form is either left to wither or subjected to attempted mutation. There is no unfolding, no outward volution, no growth and articulation of form, but barren stagnation and perversion of meaning and purpose as its nature is violated. One is thus said to operate from the periphery, and teetering on this existential edge unable to tap the inexhaustible core of being.

As central being is truth, peripheral being is a perversion of truth. As central being is freedom and divergent abandon, peripheral being is a banishment to a personally meaningless wasteland where the seed of one's being is left to desiccate. As central being moves to cultivate form, peripheral being moves to violate form by attempting to mutate or change it into what it is not. As we explore ever more thoroughly the nature and profound ramifications of peripheral being, the more it comes to light as the root cause of human disorder.

V

The Cultivation and Obscuration of Form

The unitive movement of love tends to the perfection of form, or the cultivation of its individuality. This love is selfless because there is no confusion of oneself with the finite object. The finite object is object qua object, the thing in itself, recognized and accepted for its limitations or definition and not one's idea of what it should be. Since the ontological status of the finite object or thing known is contingent upon its relationship to the knowing subject or conscious Self - in other words, since the Self knows the object by giving itself to it - it would be more appropriate to describe the unitive movement of love as *egoless* rather than selfless, for true recognition and acceptance of intrinsic form involves the noninsinuation of the empirical ego with its personal agenda into the life or existence of the object. For purposes of linguistic parsimony and consistency we will continue to speak of selfless love as long as this distinction is kept in mind.

The cultivation of individuality begins with the recognition and acceptance of individuality, or the clear and accurate articulation of form in both its actual and potential aspects. It is only within this delineated framework that we discover the conditions for the growth and development of the object as such, for it is impossible to cultivate form without knowing what it is. This act of cultivation is the movement of the liberated spirit, for it is an act of selfless love that tends to the liberation of the spirit in the object thus loved. In the stark relief of illumination, the uniqueness of the finite object is revealed. As a given, as a form in nature, it is essence, and if nurtured properly essence burgeons as form unfolds in a process of outward volution. It is only through this process that true freedom and happiness are to be found.

Whereas the unitive movement of love tends to the perfection of form, the separative movement of love tends to the possession of form. The separative movement is a selfish love in that it looks not to cultivate form, but to control, subjugate, or otherwise violate its nature. The ego insinuates its way into the life or existence of the finite object by attempting to shape, mold, or mutate it into something it is not. Individuality is not respected, and the uniqueness and fundamental nature of form becomes obscured. Shrouded thus, it cannot be cultivated, and its being or existence becomes inauthentic. The spirit in the form is obstructed from expression, and so the capacity for any true freedom and fulfillment is clipped.

Cultivating individuality or uniqueness of form is an act. It is an act of engaging form that flows naturally from the clear recognition and acceptance of its uniqueness. The nature of this act of engagement inheres in its orientation to form, or its particular manner or mode of movement in relation to the finite object. In the most direct descriptive sense, we may say that the unitive movement of love, in its inter-relationship with form, moves *with* form, or *goes with* the limitations of the finite object. It is easy to misrepresent this attitude as mere passivity, as some laissez-faire mindset. This confusion leads to profound misunderstanding. The *gentle way* of judo, for instance, as a most prominent example of the principle of going with, is quite active. Yet it moves with form. It uses the energy and motion of the opponent to throw him, as a sailor uses the wind to fuel and direct his ship. Far from inert passivity, moving with form is the superior order of human operation, for it is the formal basis of all art and science.

The artist works with the limitations of his medium. The Chinese calligrapher, with respect for the inherent qualities of brush, ink, and paper, develops a pace or flow in his strokes that is neither too fast, lest the ink streak, nor too slow, lest it smudge. The beauty of the art lies not in the calligraphy alone, but in the joyous freedom of movement and expression found within the limitations or definition of the medium. In other instances the criteria for moving with form are less visible and concrete, and we rely on abstract and subjective aesthetic standards to let us know when a medium is violated. There are no yardsticks or mathematical formulae for this. Yet a true materialist, one who truly loves matter, and not the sense of omnipotence that comes from possessing it, reflexively recoils with a sense of offense at the disrespect for the natural configuration of form. Despite the truism that taste is purely subjective, there certainly are acts of objective vulgarity. Although there is no definitive, articulated rule of aesthetics that dictates the difference between dignifying form and disgracing it, with only a modicum of sensitivity and intelligence we know it when we see it. Uniqueness is not cultivated, but violated. This is the separative movement of love that moves against form, that negates its inherent qualities in the quest to subjugate, control, or otherwise possess it.

The principle of moving with also inheres in the evolution and development of scientific theory and research. The very premise of science is to understand the nature of the universe, including and especially ourselves. We begin, in principle, with form, and seek to understand it for what it is, for its nature. We construct theories to help us understand form in both its inner relations and its relations with other forms. Our theories must be internally consistent, to satisfy our intellectual aesthetics, and empirically referenced, or substantiated by facts, so as not to be relegated to the status of fanciful ideas or science fiction. History is replete with powerful examples of empirical data growing inconsistent with preexisting theory, forcing scientists into the crisis of either blindly holding to their old paradigms or "going with the flow" as entirely new and unfamiliar systems of thought are ushered into the scientific community (Kuhn 1962). At this juncture science can solidify into intellectual orthodoxy or doctrine, or it can embody the act of perfecting form through the cultivation of intellectual truth. It can be subjected to petrifaction or properly nurtured in a living environment of development and change. The inestimable profundity of the principle of moving with is suggested by imagining the incredible fortitude involved in relinquishing a scientific *Weltanschauung* that has been the integrative thread of one's life, thought, and identity. But aside from intellectual and spiritual death, there is no other way, for as with music, we either grow with it or it will grow without us.

The unitive movement of love engages form by going with it, by recognizing and accepting its individuality, and thus acting to cultivate it. The principle of cultivating form is most eloquently expressed in its application to finite objects that *evolve*, specifically in the ontogenetic sense. We classify such objects as *organic*, for the natural course of their individual existences is to burgeon or unfold, not randomly, but in accordance with the seed of individuality that is given. This process of unfolding must be considered a temporal event, for like a bag gradually turned inside out, the central and intrinsic attributes of the object are manifested later in time. To cultivate organic form is thus to set the proper conditions for its outward volution, or the growth and development of the object as such. This outward volution can only proceed from the object's center of being, *authentically*, or along the lines of its particular nature. Any movement or development that is not intrinsically rooted, that is strictly peripheral or inauthentic, inevitably culminates in existential stagnation and spiritual death.

From the standpoint of the present discussion, the organic form that most concerns us is the human infant. Liberating the spirit in this form through the cultivation of its individuality is the key to personal happiness and freedom, and, in turn, to a greater measure of social stability and integration. Spiritual repletion, by its natural expression in a unitive movement of love, carries profound implications on the individual and supra-individual level. This is not to espouse a utopian philosophy, however. Extreme liberalism would hold that people who commit egregious acts are necessarily sick, mentally ill, or morally immature and deficient. It has become intellectually retrogressive to suggest that someone can simply be bad, and the very use of the word *evil* invokes notions of melodrama and religious fundamentalism. The legal assessment of mental deficiency is gauged by the ability to distinguish right from wrong. If the wrongdoer is unable to make this distinction, or unable to understand the effects of his actions on others, indeed he is deficient. But what if he can distinguish? What if he knows, in objective terms, that the act is legally or morally wrong - that he will be punished if caught, and that it will certainly hurt another person, and yet uncaringly performs it anyway? Grandmothers and traditional folk are allowed to diagnose such a person as "mean spirited" or "just plain bad." Academics and intellectuals, especially mental health professionals, are expected to be more responsible in their thinking. Yet our core institutional structures are predicated on the distinction between sick and bad, for there are mental hospitals and there are prisons. Disquieting as it may be, there is a principle of evil that relativizes the good. Is the recidivist and incurable sociopath who is unresponsive to any therapy or medication "suffering from" a gross deficiency in the capacity for guilt and empathy? Or is it that he has no soul? Perhaps we may say that sick people do bad things in spite of themselves, whereas bad people do bad things *because* of themselves. Because there are bad people, whether their individuality is cultivated or not, they will continue to introduce disorder into the social order. The utopian ideal is but an abstraction, an attempt to make the good absolute. But along with disorder as a "necessary evil" are the educational and healing arts that can be profoundly prophylactic and curative. The cultivation of human individuality is one of them.

We begin with the human infant and its unique genetic constitution. As soon as its constituent gametes meet and form a zygote, the blueprint is laid for a host of physical and psychological features. The eventual color and texture of one's hair, shape of the fingernails, adult height, set point for weight, predisposition for certain diseases, and the like, are all implied or "encoded" by the uniquely varying sequences of the four nucleotides comprising the DNA strands. This is not to say that environment has no impact on genetics. Chromosomes can be damaged or mutated by environmental toxins, and the natural expression of the gene can be altered or hindered by sociocultural formations, as in the traditional Chinese practice of binding feet to keep them from their preordained size. But the basic configuration is most certainly a given, in the nature of things, and like no other.

This basic configuration or blueprint goes beyond the physical determinations to include matters of character and personality. The idea of the infant as a piece of clay waiting to be molded is not only scientifically naïve, but a product of extraordinary hubris. It proceeds from the identification of the human ego with God, such that *man* creates man in his own image. That which is given is not sacred, but to be negated or subjugated by the ego, typically for its own glorification. With this presumption of godliness the universe becomes devoid of meaning, as there is nothing for the ego to love and respect other than its own reflections.

For more than forty years it has been well documented that infants intrinsically differ in terms of basic temperamental characteristics, and the wider research underscoring the genetics of personality is ample (Eaves, Eysenck, and Martin 1989; Eysenck 1967; Plomin and McClearn 1993; Thomas and Chess 1977). Parents of two or more children typically marvel at how different they are despite common genetic and environmental stock. Ironically, the most obvious fact is also the most elusive, for we simply need to remind ourselves that they are, after all, different people. The tabula rasa model denies the creative power of God by making man the chief architect of human personality. Some of us may wonder why it is that two people will respond differently to the same or similar circumstances. Why, for example, will one person who was beaten as a child beat his own children, whereas another will adopt a philosophy of nonviolence? Is the variance in these personalities simply a function of how they were molded? This would reduce personality and character to purely extrinsic contingencies that both shape and constitute the human soul. In this formulation there is nothing *in* and *of* the person that is given, that processes and responds to these contingencies in its own way, and affects them accordingly. The study of the individual in society becomes a study in molding or programming, ignoring the element of intrinsic individuality that unremittingly engages social information in a dialectical process. To deny that things have their own nature is the kind of absolute egocentrism that lifts us, like Icarus, to dangerous heights of grandiosity. Man *as ego* cannot become God by hopelessly striving for omnipotence. Man as one with the Infinite Self *is* God, manifesting omnipotence through the creation and perfection of the finite order.

We are taught that all people are created equal, or are equal in the eyes of God. The truth of this edict lies in the idea that from the standpoint of the Infinite, everything has its eternal significance. From the finite and relative standpoint, however, people are far from equal. Some are clearly smarter, stronger, healthier, or better looking. A particular talent or aptitude, for example, is a gift. One is born with it, "out of the gate," as they say. We know this because of less talented others who never achieve the same level of excellence or mastery in a given discipline despite the amount of time and effort invested. To deny the reality of talents and aptitudes is to soar ever higher with wings of wax.

Whether a particular gift is recognized and cultivated is independent of the fact of its existence. The popular slogan that "a mind is a terrible thing to waste" is painstakingly true, for the likelihood is great that unusual talents and aptitudes often go unnoticed. It would not stretch the limits of credibility to suggest that there is a potential Einstein or Mozart shrouded by the hopelessness and crime infestation of an inner-city housing project, the famine and pestilence of a Third World country, or the self-absorption of a derelict parent. As with most resources, the problem does not lie in their alleged dearth, but in their not being acknowledged.

With a profound surge of epistemic curiosity, the developing child needs a stimulus-rich environment in which to explore and express freely. In a world of computers, musical instruments, paints and brushes, tools of sport and craft, and books on every topic, free exploration is the process of expansively sampling this world, availing oneself of its wondrous offerings. Through this process, the mysterious principle of individuality is manifested, for *without any cues or direction from without,* natural inclinations or interests emerge in relation to particular areas of subject matter. We may say that these interests are innate, for they are arrived at freely, without demand or imposition, or even any significant life experience. In this act of pure will, we see mirrored in the world of finite objects the inmost depths of one's individuality and soul. Yet free exploration and the discovery of natural inclinations is not enough. The child must be able to engage the areas of subject matter that interest him, and thereby express himself freely. By manifesting himself in a particular medium, whether music, sports, science, or art, the foundation is laid for the discovery of particular aptitudes and talents. We may say that these talents and aptitudes, as defined, are also innate, for without training or practice children differ in their facility with respective disciplines, both upon initial encounter and in their capacity to improve. Through a process of social comparison the child sees his expression relative to others, and forms tentative sensibilities regarding his strengths. When these strengths are recognized and clearly reflected by discerning adults, they solidify into a definitive awareness of not only one's interests, but of one's talents and aptitudes as well.

Discerning one's own ideas, or thinking for oneself, also proceeds from free exploration and expression. The cornerstone of intellectual freedom is the ability to triangulate, and thus engage information as part of an ongoing dialectical process. Thinking divergently, or questioning, places ideas in their larger epistemological context. In so doing, any intellectual position or thesis is richly juxtaposed to antitheses, thus creating the necessary tension for a resolution in the form of a free and informed commitment to an idea, attitude, or philosophy. One may continue to embrace thesis and reject antithesis, embrace antithesis and reject thesis, or transcend the two by deriving a third principle of synthesis. This process may continue until the individual, at least for the time being, comes to a position that "sits well" with him, or is consonant with his larger intellectual, emotional, and intuitive structure. Again, the ineffable principle of individuality is manifested, for *without imposition, demand, or officious guidance*, ideas are freely derived or crystallized in an expansive field of intellectual data. One is not told how or what to think, for the thought process is neither preempted nor truncated. Why it is that individuals with intellectual latitude differ in the conclusions they draw and the positions they adopt cannot be reduced to experiential contingencies, for we know that people with similar experiences or circumstances do not all think alike. The mystery of the given must be invoked, not as a problem to be solved but as a reality to be experienced.

With the clear articulation and unreserved acceptance of the child's freely derived talents, aptitudes, interests, and ideas, the individual qua individual, pristine and unique, is ushered into the world of social discourse. The authentic self, both actual and potential, is now regnant in the minds of significant socializing personnel, and like a seed in fertile soil, properly positioned for cultivation. The act of cultivation, like so many of the profundities of the human process, is actually an art of the utmost simplicity, for it is not intended to create or change anything, but rather to facilitate a naturally occurring process. This natural process is organic form tending toward and proceeding with its own outward volution, or the ongoing exteriorization of its inmost fundamental properties. This process is said to proceed from one's center of being because it represents authenticity, and must be distinguished from the more peripheral development that is guided by false interests and ambitions. No matter how accomplished one may be in a given discipline or field of endeavor, if it is personally meaningless we can speak only of stagnation and not growth.

When we speak of facilitating a naturally occurring process, or the growth and development of the object as such, we are neither engaging in contradiction nor soliciting redundancy. Man as homo sapien is also *homo socius* (Berger and Luckmann 1966), a social creature by his very being. Just as it is in the nature of the individual to evolve along certain lines, so it is in the nature of the process of evolving to need nurturance or a facilitating social environment. This is not to deny that there are those with an unusually strong sense of self who manifest their individuality despite the absence of such facilitation, for there are always children who are either forced to raise themselves, or fight the oppression of externally imposed ambitions and modes of expression. Yet human development implies its context, social or otherwise, and anomalies aside, proceeds optimally when the integral elements of the situation are in harmony.

The outward volution of what we consider organic form, far from entropic, is a process of the highest order of meaning and intelligence. The idea that it is intrinsic to the organism to develop along certain lines immediately precludes any notion of randomness, and instead points to the same intelligence that inheres in the movement of the entire universe. Western culture is so accustomed to equating intelligence exclusively with the linear-sequential process of human thought that it fails to realize that the brain, which underlies human thought, does not in itself conform to the principle of linearity. Instead, the brain and organism as a whole, as a manifestation or expression of the universe as a whole, operate on the principle of *simultaneity*, wherein an indefinite multiplicity of highly complex processes occur at the same time (Watts 1957). Linear thought and its entrance into the time series proceeds from the kaleidoscope of rich and unceasing simultaneity that is the ever-present moment. It is a critical faculty and necessary to survival, yet when elevated to the status of a superior form of intelligence it is but one step away from being considered the only form of intelligence. To suggest that the foundation and context of the human intellect are of a lesser order of intelligence is ultimately to suggest that the intelligence of man arises ex nihilo, from an otherwise stupid universe.

Is it not the ultimate anthropocentric position to suggest that human intelligence is of a higher order than that of the "smaller-brained" creatures, such as birds and gerbils? We are amazed to discover that an eagle can soar for hours without a flap of his wings. We see a gerbil adroitly position a shell in front of his mouth, scissor through it with his teeth, release the seed, and discard the shell, and are amazed by his speed and pinpoint accuracy. If we blink we can miss it. But alas, as amazing as all this is, it is not intelligence proper, but instinct. The foundation for this distinction is that man, more than any other creature, has a predominantly *open* relationship with his social and physical environment. His activity, in other words, is only partly constituted by reflex and preconfigured response patterns to specific triggers or stimuli, and largely a function of conscious or unconscious deliberation against a backdrop of socially instituted codes of conduct and communication (Berger and Luckmann 1966). Yet reflective thought and sociocultural guidelines are linear formations that are products of an organic brain, of which linear thought is just one function. The brain itself, while enduring through time, does not operate linearly, but on the obvious principle of simultaneity, as it at once "coordinates" the manifold regulatory processes of the body and its complex transactions with the environment. In traditional terms, the brain that makes linear thought possible operates instinctively, for it does not need to run through a series of thoughts, plans, and intentions before it digests food, grows a new tooth, or even runs through a series of thoughts, plans, and intentions. By circumspectly revisiting some old and familiar ontological categories, we see that the line between instinct and intelligence is illusory. We discover the world of instinct as a different form of intelligence, comprehensive and profound, of which linear intellectualism is but a facet. To attribute unintelligence to the very organicity responsible for linear intellectualism is one step from attributing unintelligence to the very universe that produces and sustains intelligent organicity. This is clearly an oxymoron, invoking the reminder that something cannot come from nothing. Moreover, it can make us feel like carbon-based freaks in a universe that is alien and chaotic, one that generates fear and hostility, and thus the drive to dominate and control it. This is clearly not a good situation.

How, then, does one facilitate intelligent process? Conceivably, we could develop a highly elaborate theoretical and practical approach to the art of facilitation, replete with general principles, specific rules, and methods of application. Yet this would only serve to complicate a simple phenomenon, the effectiveness of which derives from the very beauty and elegance of its simplicity. Moreover, applying theory and formulae introduces so much methodology that the performance anxiety of "getting it right" is likely to place the caregiver in a state of heightened *self*-consciousness, thus stealing the spotlight from the child. Naturally this could constitute a severe impediment to the expression of self*less* love needed for the cultivation of form. And this is the answer to our question. One facilitates an intelligent process through an act of selfless love, the nature of which is to move with the process. The Taoists speak of "getting behind and gently pushing" (Watts 1957), which is not to set the direction of the movement, but to support and encourage it, much like a strong dancer supporting the movements of a tentative partner who has been asked to take the lead. This is not the adoption of a laissez-faire attitude that gives carte blanche to the child. Noninterference is not disengagement, for the process of evolving is a natural event in a social being in a social context, and thus a natural aspect of the event is the fact of human facilitation. True autonomy, in other words, must be mirrored, and respecting the nature and direction of the movement does not mean abandoning it.

To the narcissist the principle of selfless love may be superficially understood and even proclaimed as an ideal, but putting it into practice is another issue. Acknowledging the finite object as is, in this instance, recognizing the innate talents and interests of the child, can be a difficult proposition. Remaining attuned to the inherent directionality of the object's movement and unfolding, shadowing it and gently pushing it, can be impossible. Narcissistic functioning is a form of psychological myopia wherein consciousness is affixed to one's own ego. One is also conscious of other matters and people, but principally in terms of how they can be subordinated to this ego for the purpose of ongoing validation and aggrandizement.

In this regard, the narcissistic caregiver generally falls into one of two modes of dereliction. The first is simple neglect. The child, in this instance, is experienced as an inconvenience and an attentional threat, competing with the immature narcissism of the adult for a spot in the limelight. Since the premier consideration and agenda of the narcissist are the social drama of self-exaltation, anything or anyone undermining this process must be dismissed. Still in the service of ego-enhancement, compensatory face-saving measures (Goffman 1959) must then be implemented to cloak such unbecoming exclusionary tactics, the most common of which is to subsume them euphemistically under the rubric of "laissez-faire parenting." Whatever it is called, the ultimate meaning is singularly known in the effect it has on the child, which is abject isolation and the consequent impoverishment of self-concept and self-esteem.

The second mode of dereliction is to use the child for psychological gain by subordinating his individuality to the agenda of the narcissistic ego. The child, in this instance, is primarily a means to an end, which is to gratify a compensatory esteem need for the adult. A man who feels shame over disappointing his physician father for not becoming a physician himself may foist this vocation on his own son, making the child's very reason for being and anticipated success a vehicle to reflect positively on himself. "Look at what *my* son accomplished." Is this truly loving the finite object, the other, or simply the gratification of personal vindication? The contents of this scenario can be as varied as there are such instances of relationship, but the basic form is the act of imposing one's own definition on the child and directing the nature of the movement accordingly. The child as such is more of a project than an object, and while ostensibly showered with attention, is essentially overlooked. This is as negligent as outright neglect, but it is more insidious. The narcissistic adult seems to be a proponent of the child ("I'm doing all of this for *you*"), but is really trying to solidify his own fragile esteem in this act of spiritual and psychological rape.

As a form in and of the natural world, the fundamental character or personality of the individual, in both its actual and potential aspects, is perfect unto itself, in its uniqueness. Inseparable from its social context, it can either be cultivated or subjugated. In these modes of dereliction we see the separative movement of love as it engages form by moving against it. That which is given is not sacred. Individuality is not respected, but negated or subjugated by the insinuative ego of the narcissistic adult. Uniqueness of form, in terms of the innate talents, aptitudes, interests, and ideas of the child, is not clearly articulated but obscured. There is thus no outward volution of the authentic self, but only the stagnation of peripheral development, the movement of which is either randomly derived or directed by the imposition of extrinsic interests and ambitions. This subjugation of individuality is the foundation of depression and anxiety, the hallmarks of human disorder, and is responsible for the despair and meaninglessness of existential alienation and spiritual impoverishment. Although, as noted, there are always those with an unusually compelling sense of self who can manifest their individuality despite the absence of appropriate facilitation, this is the exception rather than the rule.

The idea of the individual as a constitutionally unique being means that the true form or personality cannot be destroyed by bad parenting since it was not created by parenting in the first place. It is a given, in the nature of things, and parenting can either work with it or against it. When working with, parenting cultivates the form, or allows for its fullest articulation and expression. When working against, parenting does not destroy the form, but rather obscures its recognition and thereby limits its manifestation.

VI

Peripheral Being and Human Disorder

To thine own self be true. Never has an edict cut so incisively to the root of human disorder. When one's thoughts, emotions, interests, and talents are ill defined, programmed, conflicted, or otherwise negated, one does not know oneself in order to be true to it. When one's self-concept is distorted and self-esteem reduced, that which is given or innate in personality and character becomes hopelessly shrouded. This state of existential alienation or inauthenticity is the hollow reality of peripheral being. We will attempt to show that the preponderance of human disorders, spiritual, psychological, and physical, are founded upon this unfortunate condition.

The factors that contribute to the subjugation of individuality and the consequent precipitation of human disorder are twofold in origin. One set of factors is rooted in the general culture and transmitted to the child principally through parents or caregivers as primary socializing personnel. These consist of maxims, aphorisms, clichés, truisms, allegories, and proverbs, all of which are programmed "thought bytes" that are planted in consciousness and act as cognitive vises. Since they are hardened forms or templates, they do not stimulate thought, but limit and mold it, sustaining a measure of social uniformity of consciousness. The other set of factors is rooted in the idiosyncrasy of the particular family, and also transmitted by primary socializing personnel. We refer here to the complex cognitive, affective, and behavioral social field of interaction comprising the politics of the family, for as a negative form its potential damage to psychological development is inestimable. Neither set of factors is completely distinguishable from the other, for cultural platitudes are always transmitted with a personal twist, and idiosyncratic family dynamics are always and necessarily ensconced in a cultural context. The distinction is in the respective weights or contributions of the general and the specific.

Probably the most profound and compelling example of socially conditioned consciousness stomping on the process of individuation is the effect of cultural negativity on the aspirations of the vocational self, the fulfillment of which is one of the cornerstones of cultivated individuality. We will explore this issue in some detail, and then move on to the taboo arena of the politics of the family.

Negativity and the Death of Aspiration

Among the prototypical experiences of childhood is for one to be exposed to the laments of forlorn adults who feel they missed their calling in life. Bored and unfulfilled in their work, they typically relish any opportunity to escape into conversation about forsaken dreams. The despairing waitress, for example, has been known to utter such declarations as, "I always wanted to be a dancer, but somehow I ended up serving coffee." Without yet the taint of cultivated cynicism, a child hearing this will typically and reflexively think or ask, "So how come you're not dancing?"

Of course it is possible that the woman in this example has no talent whatsoever, and that the child's question is of no practical value for her life. But what if she has talent? What if she is a potential genius? Then the question of why she is not dancing is no mere ingenuous query, but perhaps the most important question in her life.

It is all too easy to underestimate the significance of the fact that most people are lost vocationally. The expressions on the faces of those heading to work in the morning reflect this truth, and it is not surprising that the majority of heart attacks seem to take place on Sunday nights and Monday mornings. Disenchanted and uninspired by a lack of meaningful connection to their work, these alienated souls eagerly await the end of the day and week, vacation, and even retirement, not realizing that they are wishing their lives away. The reality of the present moment brings no fascination or joy, and relief is found in the anticipation of "happy hour," when the masses retreat to their favorite watering holes to lose themselves in the agitated distraction of superficial social discourse, loud music, sardonic complaints about work, and, of course, the numbing effects of alcohol. All this because they are not doing what they want.

For fear of appearing childish and naïve we are pressured, at this point, to squelch the obvious question. The "adult" attitude is to take this substandard vocational situation as a given, as an example of the harsh realities of life and the imperfection of the human condition. Yet behind the self-conscious posturing of assumed maturity, and clouded by the anticipated embarrassment of a patronizing smile, we are tempted to ask, "Well, why? Why are they not doing what they want?" If we suspend our cynicism even for a moment and seriously consider the question, we can see it for its utter profundity and power.

The key to the answer lies in the heart of the question. Its presupposition is that people can and should be fulfilled, and that it is a curious situation when they are not. It naturally assumes that outcomes will be favorable, and skepticism is both alien and remote. The adult reaction to this view is that it is immature idealism. The innocent consciousness has yet to be saved and wrested from the heartbreaks and disappointments that come from having high hopes. We are encouraged not to set our sights too high, and the general mindset is that wonderful outcomes are likely not to occur. In short, inspiration is met with discouragement, and dreams are quickly shattered. And this is the answer to our question. Negativity is the death of aspiration.

The hallmark of negativity is that it is insidious. Like Beelzebub, it cloaks itself in many forms and hides behind many masks. It infiltrates our consciousness with great stealth, seizing control of a powerful ship and harnessing tremendous energy for its own ends. Sometimes it disguises itself as a benign admonition, a piece of advice from a well-meaning friend who wants us to be realistic, stay grounded, and keep our heads out of the clouds. Going deeper, it works its way into our commonplace philosophizing and basic aphorisms. Many of us, in moments of great enthusiasm and ambition, have been recipients of such classics as, "You can't eat your cake and have it too," "Be happy you're not on the street," and "You have to live in the real world." Even our cultural icons, some of whom fancy themselves libertarians and iconoclasts free from social conditioning, unwittingly convey negativity in their words and images. As the Rolling Stones remind us, "You can't always get what you want, but if you try sometime, you just might find, you get what you need" (Jagger and Richards 1969). Others have similarly advised "if you can't be with the one you love, love the one you're with" (Stills 1970).

It is a simple fact of survival that we need to see our enemy objectively in order to defend ourselves from it. Messages that are subliminal are far more persuasive than messages that are supraliminal, or conscious (Bowers 1984; Erdelyi 1985; Erdelyi and Goldberg 1977; Silverman 1983). When the information is "behind" us, it pushes us around, manipulating our thoughts, emotions, and actions as if we were automata. When it is in front of us, when it is the thing *known,* we can distinguish ourselves from it and thus gain the freedom to operate on our own terms. If we suspend our cynicism long enough to look at negativity objectively, it loses status in the real world. Far from realism, negativity as a point of view is seen to be more tentative than definitive. As its infrastructure erodes, so lessens its hypnotic grip on our consciousness.

The irreducible measure of the substance of a philosophy is its pragmatic component, or usefulness. As speculation and theory, philosophy offers endless hours of rich thought and discussion. When incorporated into the body of daily life it becomes an instrument for transformation, the ultimate value of which is its ability to augment the quality of this life. It is not entirely true, therefore, to say that knowledge is power. It would be more correct to say that knowledge *applied* is power. Otherwise it is mere entertainment.

The most popular application of the principle of negativity is the attempt to protect oneself from the pain of disappointment. So often we hear people say, "I expect the worst and hope for the best. This way when bad things happen I'm not disappointed, and when good things happen I'm pleasantly surprised." The problem with this mindset is twofold. The first is that when bad things happen we are disappointed anyway. The second is the mindset itself. Aside from being downright depressing, it is dangerous. Do we really want to live in a subjective universe where the worst is expected? If psychology has taught us anything, it is that attitude and expectancy play a significant role in the determination of outcome (Ajzen1988; Fishbein and Ajzen 1975). In much the same way, a car will move in the direction the driver is looking. Trite as it may be to say, we certainly do fulfill our own prophecies. If we do not embrace this philosophy, we must confront the abject horror of an existence that is purely determined, either by the preexisting script of Calvinism or the random and fortuitous forces of a meaningless universe.

A look at the validity of negativity as a philosophy or viewpoint is important as well. Something is deemed valid when it makes sense, or is rational, and can be seen in the world, or is empirical. From the rational standpoint, the ultimate expression of negativity is rooted in the philosophy of nihilism. The job of the nihilist is to negate. What his myopic philosophizing prevents him from seeing is that the act of negation, *being an act*, is actually an affirmation. It is something in the world. He fails to understand that by saying "Nothing exists," this must include the very statement and the one who utters it. If the statement does not exist, then its proposition is meaningless. If the one who utters it does not exist, then certainly we do not have to acknowledge him, at least in his capacity as philosopher.

From the empirical standpoint we see a world of human design resplendent with invention, creation, and discovery. When many of these realities were still merely prescient ideas, they evoked accusations of heresy and madness against those who conceived them. Society, it is often said, kills its prophets. But the fact remains that dreams and fantasy become reality. In 1966 there first appeared a television show called *Star Trek.* Along with its many wonders, on the bridge of the Starship Enterprise was a "most fascinating" computer. It responded to speech, and could access all and any information in a matter of moments. A mere forty-four years later, which in the course of human history is but a blink, we have voice activation and the Internet. All we need do is look at the world around us and at history to see countless other examples. Science fiction predates science, and visions evolve into technology. This clearly vindicates the idealism of the child, and against the backdrop of human accomplishment the voice of negativity sounds tinny.

Alongside the love we feel for those closest to us, at the center of our being is the *vocational self.* As discussed, this is the piece of us that is naturally drawn to certain interests and occupations. In the same way that we cannot help adoring those whom we love, we do not choose these interests and occupations. Instead, they call to us, which is why we speak of a calling and not a choosing. Even if it is never actualized, the vocational self is ever vital, and remains with us until we die. When the vocational self is not realized in the world, negativity is the murderer. Negativity manifests itself, in this regard, in three fundamental ways.

First and most simply, a child is negated when ignored. Derelict parents who fail to acknowledge and cultivate their children's talents and interests essentially banish them to a wasteland of self-anonymity, to grow into adults who are confused or diffuse in their vocational identities. More telling than the fact that most people do not *do* what they want is that they do not even *know* what they want. Struggling to see themselves in a steamy mirror, they are the first to assert that being lost is far from paradise.

43

Second and more insidiously, a child is negated when the vocational self is preempted or overwritten. This is the dereliction of subjugating individuality for personal gain. A vocational role, in other words, is ascribed to the child, typically on the basis of a parent's unfulfilled aspirations or the weight of a family tradition. How often it is that the otherwise aspiring writer is subverted and forced to join the ranks of a long line of lawyers or doctors. This is spiritual rape, with the individual qua individual virtually irrelevant and regarded as a mere mannequin to be draped with other people's clothes.

There are those with a strong enough sense of self who can emerge from the clouds and occlusions of negation and declare who they are, what they love, and what they want to do. They know, in Carlos Castañeda's (1968) words, the *path with heart*. It is at this juncture that we see the third form of negation, which is ridicule. As a form of negativity, and true to form, ridicule is more effective when insidious. It need not be so blatant as harsh criticism and insults. It can be benign. It can be advice from family and friends who look to protect us from disappointment, who gently remind us that what we want is not practical, too difficult and competitive, and not secure. We should get real jobs, become realistic, and keep our central interests as hobbies. Even when our dreams are supported, there is usually the caveat that we should have something to fall back on, which implies doubt in the successful outcome.

In the face of such negativity, the act of declaring oneself can be intimidating. The bold statement "I am a writer" or "I want to be a dancer" is typically met with discouragement. Depending on the nature, context, and severity of the ridicule, declaring oneself to others can border on the taboo. If the pressure is sufficiently compelling, declaring oneself to *oneself* can become taboo as well. In the first instance, the vocational self is choked verbally. In the second, it is strangulated psychologically, and remains as nascent ideas shadowed on the precipice of consciousness. Either way, the vocational self is forsaken, and supplanted by the nightmare of an existence that lacks authenticity.

It is at this point in our discussion that the negativist has sufficient ammunition to interject with a full arsenal of sanctimony and self-congratulatory rapture. Miming the violinist, he will sarcastically lament the plight of the existentially inauthentic, comparing them to those who are riddled with starvation and disease and living under the worst of circumstances. To this argument there are three critical objections.

The first is that it is a grave error to confuse relative pain with absolute pain. Speaking in the first person, if my arm is severed from my torso, naturally I will be in searing pain. If my friend has *two* arms severed, I would imagine that his pain is greater than mine. But the fact that his pain is greater, relatively speaking, does not diminish mine in absolute terms. I suffer the same amount whether he has two arms, one, or none. The best example of this confusion, and perhaps the platitude par excellence, is the time-honored "There's always someone who has it worse," typically evoked in response to another's suffering or dissatisfaction. Yet this attempt to comfort goes only so far, for in the words of Arlo Guthrie (1967), "What do you say to the last guy?"

The net effect of comparing pain is not to comfort us, but to shame us into not acknowledging that we have needs, wishes, and dreams. We are made to feel guilty for wanting more, for aspiring, and we are told that we complain too much and are never satisfied. We are made to feel that if our experience is less than optimal, somehow this will vindicate the suffering of others. The interesting irony is that when we forsake the very opportunities and privileges others may never have, we actually make a mockery of their suffering, for surely they would trade places with us in a heartbeat. If anything vindicates suffering it is certainly not more suffering, but the bringing to fruition in our lives what others cannot.

The second objection is that vocational fulfillment, as one aspect of existential authenticity, is that towards which the life process tends. Organic life is a burgeoning, or the outward volution of the most central and integral properties contained within. Being and doing who one is, turning oneself inside out, as it were, is the raison d'être of organic life. Failure to cultivate and exteriorize the vocational self is thus going against the very grain of life itself.

The third and most important objection to being shamed into accepting a substandard vocational situation is that we simply do not have to. Sadly, it is true that "the mass of men lead lives of quiet desperation," but tragically it does not have to be. Something can be done about it. In the face of a definitive situation, such as the death of a loved one, we have no choice but to accept it, lest we retreat into psychotic denial or commit suicide. Yet far fewer situations are definitive than we might imagine. What appears to be immutable often is not, but we do not realize this because negativity prevents us from seeing the solutions, or even looking for them. We resign and become fatalistic. We don paper chains believing them to be real, locking ourselves in a psychological prison.

Sometimes we unfairly doubt our abilities, and for fear of failure convince ourselves that little or nothing can be done about our situation. In other instances we may have learned a philosophy of helplessness that characterizes us as ineffectual, as but dust in the wind, and consequently clips even the thought of making an effort. Worse yet, we may believe that we are personally ill fated, as reflected in the sarcastic "it's just my luck" triggered by any disappointment. Or we may hold to Murphy's Law and the conviction that the worst outcome is statistically the most likely. In any case we face the danger of fulfilling our own prophecies. For many of us it is simply too late. We have passed our prime and missed the boat. Even if it were possible to fulfill our vision, it would take too much time, as if the time were not to pass anyway. In the abyss of despair we lament, silently reiterating, "So what's the point of even trying?"

While our prison bars are by their nature psychological, their full impact is existential. By limiting our capacity to expand, they configure the very course of our lives. Our chains are indeed paper in the sense that they are composed of thoughts and beliefs, which are ultimately mutable. For these chains to bind us and hold us down, they need not be real or true. We must simply believe that they are, and our experience will follow accordingly. This is the essence of hypnosis, and therefore any proper understanding or use of hypnosis in the practice of psychotherapy applies not to inducing hypnotic states, but rather to breaking them.

The way to gain freedom from an illusion is to objectify it, or see it for what it is. The masterful illusions of a great magician fascinate us and captivate our consciousness, but only until the trick is revealed. Then, while our curiosity is satisfied and we are engaged in the mechanics of the illusion, the hypnotic state is broken and our minds are once again our own.

The illusion in the present context is that our substandard situation is indeed immutable. This illusion is created by negative attitudes, beliefs, and ideas that have the power to bind and manipulate us when they are insidious or not known objectively. The corrective lens in front of my eye clarifies all the objects in my field of vision, but itself is not an object because it is too close. When I pull the lens away from my eye, I can now see *it* as an object too, and in so doing distinguish it from myself. Objectified thus, it no longer modifies my vision. Negativity is also a lens, except its function is not to clarify, but to deceive and distort. If I objectify it, or *cast it out,* it no longer modifies my consciousness, and this loosening of its hypnotic grip sets the stage for the most profound and fundamental freedom.

To objectify negative thoughts and beliefs, looking at them, making them known, is to distinguish them from the knowing self. Once distinguished, the self is better positioned to operate freely and on its own terms. Negativisms are no longer hidden and unchallenged, and like the distanced lens are thus weakened in their credibility and power to modify and distort.

To illustrate the principle of objectifying negativity, we return to the hypnosis of the psychological prison. From a narrow and myopic viewpoint, the prison and its limitations are real. Our situation is truly limited or hopeless, and there is little we can do about the hand we have been dealt. It is time to grow up, to face facts, to learn to live with the sobering realization that things do not always go our way. Perhaps, on some level, we can find a semblance of fulfillment in our vocational pursuits, knowing, at the very least, that it is honest work and toward some common good. The bulk of satisfaction, however, will be found in hobbies and diversions, largely substitutive, and always shadowed by the specter of what could have been. Life, at its best, is good enough, and a blend of compromise and concession is seen as the sine qua non of adaptation and functionality.

If we pull back from our myopic viewpoint and broaden and deepen our perspective, we become more discerning and receptive to stimuli that have always been present but never noticed. We become aware of an anxious guilt that gnaws at us, pointing to intimations that something is wrong, that somehow we are fooling ourselves, that our conscious convictions are tentative, and that our reality might just be an illusion. *In the moment of intimation* we feel a surge of inspirational energy and power. If we are able to indulge the moment and stay in it, our experience of this power becomes more profound. We see it clearly as ours, and at our command. If negativity does not obstruct the experience, the power presses us to act, to expand our minds, and to bring to fruition our ambitions. We discover that our prison is but a hologram, and that our limitations are largely imagined. Like an atom split asunder we break open, releasing unprecedented energy that explodes our imaginations and wills our visions into being. From a simple change in perspective we gain clarity, and in effect realize the freedom to bring ourselves into the world and transform it ever anew. Of the negativist we must then ask, "Will wonders never cease?"

The Politics of the Family

The title of this section is adopted from R. D. Laing's (1972) seminal book, for the family is indeed a political system, and the terminology is apropos. Yet the family is a political system only to the degree, and in the sense, that there is disorder. Where there is order there is the unitive movement of love, or selfless love, moving with form in the act of cultivating it. Where there is disorder there is the separative movement of love, or selfish love, moving against form in the act of subjugating and controlling it. In a social context the mutual need for subjugation and control of the other leads to intensive considerations of matters of status and authority, which are the essence of all political structures and processes. The contents of political configurations vary indefinitely, but in terms of form we see clusters of particular psychosocial dynamics.

In a political structure the premier consideration is the protection and promotion of oneself and personal interest at the expense of the other. Status and authority involve subjugation and control, and in this game of one-upmanship there is the necessary negation of the other. The politics of the family are therefore negative by definition, for the very power of the ascendant figures comes from subordinating the individuality of immediate others. The political game, with its infrastructure of competition and power, is, in the truest sense, a *zero-sum game,* for it is necessary that some lose so others may win. Within the politics of the family the cost to the losers is an absence of self-knowledge, and an existentially inauthentic life.

The quest for the power of subjugation and control that constitutes the foundation of political discourse is inevitably rooted in a sense of insecurity. The finite object, or other, is experienced as a threat, and must be overcome to preserve the integrity of the tenuous ego. This act of negative or Machiavellian power is invariably predicated upon the need to annihilate threat, an insight that can serve as a powerful tool for the recipient of subjugation.

Insecurity comes in many forms. A modestly attractive woman might be narcissistically threatened by her exceptionally beautiful daughter and the attention bestowed upon her. Immature and insufficiently parented adults who depend on their own children are fearful of losing them, and thus threatened by the possibility of their success and independence. A man of moderate means and education might be threatened by the escalating education and success of his son. A child is almost always threatened by a newborn or favored sibling, and as an adult might experience this rivalry in relation to his own children. Artists and musicians are often threatened by talented colleagues, as are athletes and academics. The poor often feel threatened by the rich, as do infertile women by those who can conceive. Uncoupled individuals have been known to be threatened by the marriage of a friend, as the unhappy are threatened by the happy. In the face of threat the insecure ego must act, for on par with the impulse to protect one's physical integrity is the impulse to protect one's psychological integrity. The threat must be crushed, and domination through the negation of individuality is the most efficient way.

The negation of individuality, as an act of domination and control, is optimally effective when two criteria are met. First, the assault on the child must be on every level of his being - principally, thought, emotion, and sensation. Second, the assault must, like the sting of a scorpion, have the capacity to render the victim defenseless. We see that the ultimate act of annihilation is to incapacitate the object and then crush it systemically and completely.

The negation of individuality on the level of cognition is, quite simply, the denial of the child's opportunity to think for himself. Thinking for oneself, or having a mind of one's own, if properly understood, is the hallmark of individuality, for any crystallized ideas, attitudes, or philosophies of the world and oneself are freely derived. We must distinguish this mindset from the merely reactionary, for any position that is *anti*establishment, *counter*cultural, or *non*conformist is not freely derived but tightly bound to and determined by convention, for its derivation is in the very fact of opposing convention. The conformist and the rebel are symptoms of the same intellectual servitude. Each must carefully monitor conventional guidelines, one to adhere to them and the other to oppose them.

The manifestation of individuality in freedom of thought is founded upon dialectical relationships with significant others. In contrast to the more didactic or autocratic relationships - those in which social information is foisted upon the child with authoritarian and punitive undertones - the dialectical relationship is a warm and loving interpersonal matrix in which the presentation of social information is intended to elicit dialogue and not stifle it. Positions or theses welcome antitheses, and within this rich and open conversational apparatus the dialectical process brings child and adult to new levels of understanding. The adult affects the child, and is also affected by the child, mutually and simultaneously. But this is no game of billiards, for billiard balls are not reciprocally transformed through their interactions. It would be more accurate to say that the child responds to the adult who is responding to the child who is responding to the adult responding to the child, and, at the same time and equally true, the adult responds to the child who is responding to the adult who is responding to the child responding to the adult. With the internalization of this ongoing dialectical relationship the child introjects the adult as a warm and encouraging stimulant to continued growth and free exploration. The introjected other is thus fully and truly integrated into the psyche of the child, for with ongoing dialectical processing the elements of freedom and individuality remain. Any information as a position or thesis is, as a matter of style and routine, embedded in its larger epistemological context of antitheses, and after a period of intellectual triangulation is either accepted, rejected, modified, or synthesized to an entirely new level of meaning. Crystallization of, and commitment to, an idea, attitude, or philosophy as a resolution to the tension of triangulation means thinking *for oneself,* without external imposition or officious guidance.

In the more didactic or autocratic relationships, social information is foisted upon the child, or imposed, in a hostile and punitive medium, in the form of injunctions, commands, and threats. In this instance there is no internalization of dialectical relationships, for the social situation is hardly dialectical and hardly a relationship. What is internalized is the imposing adult, and as an introject remains unintegrated in the psyche of the child, *in* him but not *of* him, looming high, but never integrated into a dialectical process. Indeed, the very principle of didactics discourages intellectual triangulation, as its intent is to teach the child what and how to think – that is, not to think for himself. Ideas, attitudes, and beliefs are presented with the imperative that they not be questioned, thus clipping the thought process and preempting any capacity for true resolution and commitment. Since there is no dialectic there is no freedom, and where there is no freedom there is no individuality. With the internalization of the didactic adult the child introjects, but does not integrate, an autonomous nodule of prescriptions and proscriptions, imperious in its mere presence, and always replete with implied admonitions about deviating from its script. The degree to which this introject is effective in precluding dialectical processing is the degree to which the child is subordinated to and programmed by a living entity that is internal but still foreign to himself, much like a lethal virus invading his body.

Among the ideas, attitudes, and beliefs foisted on the child are those pertaining to himself, and given the nature of the didactic exchange, which is to negate individuality, they are typically not positive and often distorted, like the amusement-park mirror. Through the principle of Cooley's (1902) *looking-glass self* or Mead's (1934) *role-taking,* in which we see ourselves as significant others see us, the child's *reflected self,* or self-concept, is typically of a lesser degree of quality than he actually is, whether on the level of physical attractiveness, intelligence, character, or general competence and likability. This rift between the perceived self and the real self is one of the more profound concepts in human psychology, for the ideas and emotions we generate, the decisions we make, and the actions we take are grounded not in who we actually are, but in how we have come to see ourselves. An attractive man who sees himself as unappealing may be unlikely to approach a shy but beautiful woman who is equally attracted to him. They might have fallen in love, married, and produced a child who significantly contributed to the world. This fateful decision not to approach her would not have been made on the basis of the individual's true self, but on his distorted self-image. In similar fashion, an intelligent woman who has been made to feel unintelligent may not apply for a graduate program in her true area of interest for fear of not being admitted. Although a perfect candidate, she forsakes her dream on the basis of misinformation. It is truly awesome to consider that a single decision can alter the course of one's life, and truly frightening that the decision can be rooted in a distorted self-concept.

Part of the process of the distorted self-concept thwarting the accomplishment of goals is the stress that is generated. Stress, in its essence, is *anxiety over the anticipation of a negative outcome.* It is the fear that something bad will happen, and that we will have no control over it. Some stress is objective and ultimately warranted, whereas most is subjective and wholly unnecessary. Objective stress stems from a negative, uncontrollable situation that we confront in the real world, such as a natural disaster or the terminal illness of a loved one. Subjective stress stems from a negative, uncontrollable situation that we create in our minds through the act of interpretation. It is a reaction to the meaning we give to events, not to the events themselves. A competent and resourceful individual, for example, who has been made to see himself as incompetent and mediocre is likely, when confronted with a new task or professional project, to interpret the prospect as overwhelming ("This is too much for me"), and anticipate failure. In reality, he is well equipped to meet and master the challenge, but he gives different meaning to the event and reacts with stress to a problem that exists in his mind only. Given the wide variety of physical and emotional diseases incurred by stress, the mere management of stress through simple attention-diversion techniques is only minimally and temporarily effective, for the stress must first occur in order to be counteracted, and the act of attention diversion can only last for so long. In the process of cultivating individuality by correcting the erroneous self-concept and other psychological distortions, new interpretive schemata are introduced that facilitate the ascription of realistic and empowering meanings to situations. The competent and resourceful individual who now sees himself as such, for example, will interpret the new task or professional project as an accomplishable challenge ("I can do this"), and rather than nervously anticipating failure will confidently anticipate success. In this instance subjective stress is mastered, for the interpreted situation that produced it is prevented from ever occurring.

The negation of individuality on the level of emotion begins with the emotional insecurity that comes from having never felt consistently, truly, or selflessly loved. The child feels inferior and unsafe in a fearful world of insecure attachments where people and relationships are tentative at best. The angst of this situation compels her to seek safety and security, and with the chronic self-doubt that accompanies low self-esteem, the most secure place is the known and familiar, or the existential fact of self-limitation. Fearfully clinging to what is in front of her, she closes her mind to possibility. A life thus lived is like an unwatered seed that withers and blows away with the wind.

With inconsistent, insincere, or selfish love the child is frequently hurt emotionally by insensitive or hostile words and deeds. If she is hurt or vulnerable for these or any other reasons, her need for this vulnerability to be held, soothed, comforted, and reassured compels her, as a social being, to bring it to the adult. So-called caregivers of the type we are describing typically reject this vulnerability, thereby compounding the hurt, insecurity, and fear. After repeated, thwarted efforts, the child learns that rendering herself vulnerable is too dangerous emotionally, and begins to construct an *antidependent defense* (Seinfeld 1990), exemplified in adult form in the declaration, "I don't depend on anybody for anything."

This antidependent defense is the nucleus for the formation of relationships that are fated to dissipation or stagnation. A common statement is "I always seem to get involved with the wrong people. Either we're incompatible, or they're married, emotionally unavailable, or fearful of commitment." Few people have such consistently bad luck; they are carefully, albeit unconsciously, choosing their partners. Upon superficial examination one might be tempted to predict that those who were hurt by cold rejection as children would, as adults, seek the company of warm and loving people capable of viable relationships. Yet these individuals are typically saddled with two powerful imperatives that preclude any possibility of intimacy with a viable partner. The first, the prime directive, is the protection of one's vulnerability through the antidependent defense, and the second is the need to cure the *bad object* of its empathic deficiency.

The individual who has consistently been hurt and rejected for her vulnerability quite naturally insulates this vulnerability and expends considerable energy protecting it. If she does not want to avoid relationships altogether and retreat into a schizoid withdrawal, neither does she want too much intimacy with another person. The right person can stir her heart, beseech her, beckon her love, and inspire her mind to hope and expectation. Yet this prospect is terrifying, for it makes her vulnerable. With the wrong person she knows she will never truly love, and therefore never truly be hurt. Antidependent women, for example, often complain that the "nice guys" are "boring," whereas the "bad boys" are "dangerous" and "exciting." In truth, the bad boys are actually quite safe, and are selected as such, for it is abundantly clear from the outset that there is no possibility of an intimate and viable relationship. Likewise, antidependent men tend to gravitate toward women whom they do not respect or know they can never love, and avoid those who truly touch them. The operant assumption, of course, is that there will be an interpersonal disappointment, that it is just a matter of time, and that something must be done to minimize the inevitable hurt. In a compelling essay, Martin Luther King, insisting on the principle of integration and not mere desegregation, likened integration to people baring their souls and touching hearts, and desegregation to people placing their hands on their shoulders, extending the arms, and touching elbows (Washington 1990). Antidependent relationships are elbow-touching relationships, designed as such, for when the axe inevitably falls, a wounded elbow is considerably less injurious than a wounded heart. Safe relationships either dissipate or stagnate, but either way, with the insulation of one's vulnerable core, there is little room for personal growth and expression.

The child who has consistently been hurt and rejected for her vulnerability typically blames herself for the mistreatment. This phenomenon may be explained both psychoanalytically and in terms of cognitive-developmental theory. According to Freud (Breuer and Freud

1895; Freud 1914, 1917, 1924), the child fears her anger toward the adult for two reasons. First, if the rage is sufficiently intense, fantasies abound over hurting or destroying the bad object. Since the adult is the child's principal source of life support, annihilation simply will not do. Second, the child fears retaliation from the adult for this anger, and simply experiencing it silently and interiorly without external expression is insufficient given the child's inescapable fantasy that the adult can read her mind. Rather than being felt and discharged, the anger is "strangulated," energetically converting to depression and anxiety, and the criticisms that ride on the wings of this anger are reflexively turned onto the ego, setting the stage for a gross impairment in self-esteem and a cognitive style that will interpret all subsequent abuse and mishaps as a function of personal responsibility and a reflection upon oneself.

From the standpoint of cognitive-developmental theory, particularly the work of Jean Piaget (1952), young children are naturally and stylistically egocentric. As the sole center of the universe, every contingency must somehow refer to oneself. Perspectival studies corroborate this principle; children at this developmental stage cannot comprehend that there are perspectives or visual angles on objects or events that differ from their own. Self-blame and denigration are not anxiety-based psychodynamic defenses, but forms of age-appropriate cognition. If there is death, abandonment, divorce, physical abuse, sexual abuse, verbal denigration, or simple neglect, it must be due to some personal deficiency that lies within the child. Irrespective of theory, the phenomenon of self-blame is the same, and it burns a hole in the otherwise healthy narcissism of the child and institutes schemata for future such interpretations.

Riddled with feelings of inferiority, as gauged exclusively by the treatment and reflections she receives from significant others, the child has an imperious need to restitute herself and her self-esteem, to prove her worth in the eyes of others and herself, to be ontologically valid. Regardless of the particular form it takes, if the empathic failure of the adult is the fault of the child and a measure of her deficiency, the ultimate vindication or act of self-restitution would be to elicit this empathy from the adult, more specifically in the form of positive reflections and love. In reality the child is questing to cure the bad object of its empathic deficiency, although to her it is she who is deficient, attempting to improve herself to win the desperately needed love that will prove her worthwhile. Since this quest is never accomplished, it leaves the child with an open-endedness, an unmastered task, more failure on top of her original feelings of inferiority. As she comes of age and moves into the world, her need to master this task persists, and people will thus be chosen and configured to set the stage for the drama to continue, with the hope that the task may eventually be mastered. The emotionally mature and available person is not needed for this drama, and is thus boring. The empathetically deficient person is needed, and the excitement comes from the prospect of "fixing" him and consequently feeling better about oneself. Again, since this task is never successfully accomplished, some individuals lock into mortal combat with their partners while others move on to the next conquest. This replication in adult relationships of the interpersonal dynamics of childhood is an illustration of Freud's (1920) repetition compulsion, which may be explained in terms of mechanism and motive. The mechanism, descriptively speaking, is the simple fact of repetition. The motive is to master something as an adult that could not be mastered in childhood, in this instance, the restitution of one's self-esteem through correcting the debilitated empathic capacity of the object. A relationship consumed by this motif is de facto a negation of individuality, since the arduous task of curing the bad object leaves little time for personal growth and expression.

Perhaps the most powerful way to negate individuality on the level of emotion is to institute conflict over feeling and expressing anger. Indeed, it has become implicitly institutional that anger is a taboo emotion. We see injunctions against it on many levels. Morally, it is reprehensible and to be feared. Since we misconstrue ourselves as savages who must constantly keep ourselves in check, ordered in spite of ourselves, even the hint of anger runs the risk of uncontrolled expression in physical violence. This moral injunction especially applies to the family, particularly the parents, and of course the dead. From the spiritual standpoint we are told by gurus that rage is a contaminant to the soul, and that to self-purify we must "clip the seed" of anger. The medical community warns us of cardiovascular disease, hypertension, strokes, and heart attacks, necessarily equating anger with screaming purple faces and bulging veins and tendons. This is a caricature of anger, and dangerously misleading. To some, to be angry means to be out of control, or to be socially indelicate. Others see it as emotionally and psychologically immature, a level of functioning beneath that of the "mature and rational adult." When expressed, it is typically met with fear, counteranger, or attempts to induce guilt.

The most nefarious and insidious use of instituting conflict over feeling and expressing anger is to render a potential victim defenseless. Like the sting of a scorpion that paralyzes its prey, robbing someone of the ability to be freely and expressly angry denies her the proper emotional base to protect her integrity. This is why in the structure and dynamics of an abusive relationship of any kind, the ongoing current of abuse, whether explicit or implicit, is intricately threaded with injunctions against anger. Like the opposable thumb and binocular vision, anger and all other emotions are evolutionarily significant in their adaptive capacity and survival value (Plutchik 1980). The adaptive value of the fight-or-flight response is self-protection. Fear stimulates us to run from danger, whereas anger stimulates us to counter it. While it is true that a fearful child has little opportunity to run from immediate others, it is also true that an angry child cannot protect herself from the physical aspect of abuse. But psychologically, *in principle*, she can. Were she to be freely and expressly angry at the bad object, directing her rage and contemptuous criticism toward the object, if not overtly at least in the domain of internal object relations, she would prevent the insult-added-to-injury of assuming the onus of deficiency as the factor responsible for the abuse. It is bad enough to be mistreated. It is worse if it is one's fault. Mistreatment would still hurt and enrage, but the deficiency responsible for this interpersonal disorder would clearly lie in the personality of the other, not oneself. But we are not allowed to be freely and expressly angry, outwardly or inwardly. Injunctions in the form of social self-consciousness and the anticipated reactions of others compel us to hide the visible signs of anger, not simply acts of aggression, but verbal expression, volume and tone of voice, hostile posturing, and that physiological state of agitated emotion called "hot under the collar." Moral injunctions, however, compel us to hide the anger not simply from others, but also from ourselves. Suppressing the visible signs of an emotion is one thing. Injunctions against even thinking or feeling it are another. In the realm of internal object relations, the child is not even allowed to be angry at the introjected object, the internalized other. Like an angry dog biting her own tail, she has no recourse but to turn a dyadic social situation into a reflexive monistic situation. She must intercept the vector of anger directed toward the bad object or the bad object representation and deflect it, like a boomerang, turning it back on herself as her own object or self-representation (Freud 1917).

This vector of anger consists of anger as an emotion, "angry" thoughts in the form of contemptuous criticism, and possibly an impulse toward physical expression. When anger as an emotion is not allowed to be felt and expressed, in terms of either contemptuous criticism or physical aggression, either toward the external object or the internal object representation, it is, in Freud's terms, strangulated or suppressed without any opportunity for discharge (Breuer and Freud 1895). We see here the genesis of anxiety and depression, plus a host of somatizations and physical disorders. When the contemptuous criticism that rides on this anger becomes reflexive, we see a morass of ongoing self-directed criticism and denigration that negatively distorts and reduces one's self-concept and self-esteem (Freud 1917). If, in the course of dialogue, we map the content of one's ideation in these instances, we see quite clearly through transposition of the self-representation and the internal object representation that the denigration directed toward oneself could, thematically, just as easily be directed to the adult. Indeed, this denigration is meant for the adult originally, but the child, for the reasons stated, sacrifices herself instead. Once she is mistreated and having deflected the reactive anger and criticism onto herself, a pattern begins wherein the child is unable to defend herself, and thus susceptible to ongoing abuse, both in childhood and beyond. As the cycle continues the abuse mounts, and in a synergistic way, for as time passes the child is not simply the recipient of the compounding abuse from without, but also the infusion of this abuse with her own self-directed reactive anger that was originally meant for the bad object. If there is an impulse toward physical aggression it is, in the face of transgression, either contained or, like contemptuous criticism, directed reflexively in the form of some kind of self-abuse, mistreatment, sabotage, or destruction. Depressed, anxious, self-loathing, responsible for her abuse and unable to defend herself, the child grows fearful of people, of being seen. As she hides her perceived characterological ugliness from the world, her energies are thus spent developing a palatable persona rather than her true personality. By negating her anger, she obstructs the cultivation of her individuality.

The negation of individuality on the level of sensation results from either the absence of physical demonstrations of love and affection from the adult, or, more obviously, the presence of physical or sexual abuse. Intuitively and academically we are impressed by how crucial a role is played by physical proximity and expressivity in the psychological, emotional, and physical well-being and development of an individual. The rejuvenating power of a hug, the emotional comfort and reassurance of a caress, the encouragement of a pat on the back, the validation of a handshake, the bonding power of a mother brushing her daughter's hair, and the cradled support of an infant securely held are all illustrations of the immeasurable power of loving, tactile contact. Anthropological and psychological research offers abundant corroboration of this intuited principle. With the implementation of instrumental functions such as feeding, inoculating, and the provision of shelter, but an absence of socioemotional expression in the forms described, human infants, such as those institutionalized, are thwarted in their human development, typically devolving into emotionally stunted adults with varying degrees of empathic deficiency and a corresponding inability to bond (Provence and Lipton 1962). The same principles and effects have been observed in nonhuman primates, from the "motherless mothers" who kill their offspring, to the preference of infant monkeys for terrycloth as opposed to wire "mothers," to the neonates who die due to a lack of tactile contact (Harlow and Harlow 1986). This principle is so fundamental that it reiterates itself in multiple contexts. A popular television commercial reminds us to hug our children. Sex therapists teach us to be more sensitive lovers by discerning differential responsiveness to touch. Psychologically oriented business consultants speak of the right and wrong kinds of handshakes. Science fiction is replete with themes of evanescent and incorporeal aliens or spirits of the dead who despairingly yearn to feel the warm caress of a summer breeze and the touch of a human hand. Again, we are *homo socius*, and the veritable indispensability of positive physical contact is not to be relegated to a lesser status than any other fundamental need.

Untouched, the child hungers. Unsecured, he feels insecure. Expressly unloved, he feels inferior. Needy, anxious, and self-doubting, he is disinclined to freely explore himself and the world. The perils of anticipated failure and isolation immobilize him, and he seeks comfort and security in the self-limitation of the known and familiar. Without a safe harbor, and lacking confidence in himself, he forfeits the unrealized seed of his being, and in its place erects a fortress of overly rationalized, self-defeating ideas and actions.

Physical abuse disrupts the individuation process for a number of reasons. First, like any bully, the abusive adult resorts to physicality because of an inability or unwillingness to engage the child in verbal discourse. Unlike the dialectical adult, the abusive adult is didactic in his issuance of commands, and the verbal medium is principally for the threats and denigration that typically accompany the inducement of pain. In the absence of dialectical exchange there is little opportunity for intellectual triangulation, and thus learning to think for oneself, which is a hallmark of individuality. Moreover, physical assaults to the body hardly constitute a loving and holding environment. Assuming all responsibility and blame, the child who is treated despicably is made to feel inferior, for physical abuse can no more build confidence and character than poisons can be blended to make an elixir. He is also made to feel insecure, for he lives in an unsafe world filled with uncertainty and fear.

And then there is rage. Rage is typically precipitated by one of two preexisting physical or emotional states. The first is frustration, well exemplified by the *frustration-aggression hypothesis* in psychological learning theory (Dollard and Miller 1950). Many of us have had the experience of being stuck behind an exceptionally slow driver on the highway. We become frustrated, and the frustration typically compels us to express ourselves aggressively and angrily, honking the horn, slamming the dashboard, screaming epithets, recklessly attempting to pass him, and exhibiting any other animated expression that may be subsumed under the popular rubric "road rage." The second precipitant of rage is pain, either as a sensation or in the form of emotional hurt. Forensic experts and laypeople alike speak of crimes of passion. Although the perpetrators are typically not sociopaths and feel horrible and insufferable remorse after the fact, in the heat of the moment they are actually quite vicious. Betrayal, infidelity, abandonment, deception are all enough to induce the worst emotional hurt or pain, and then the rage that overwhelms us in acts of violence and murder. Physical pain in itself can be a precipitant of rage, as some of us may have had the experience of stubbing a toe and wanting to kick the object, or banging our head on a cabinet door and then angrily slamming it. It is often said, in this regard, that there is nothing more dangerous than a wounded animal. With physical abuse there is typically pain as a sensation coupled with emotional hurt, igniting the worst kind of rage. It is at this juncture that we revisit the problem of exteriorizing anger, or directing it toward the object or object representation. The most common outcome, due to fear and injunctions against anger, is not to exteriorize the rage, but to suppress the emotion and redirect the contemptuous criticism onto one's own self-representation, resulting in depression, anxiety, and self-loathing. In considering the conditions necessary for the cultivation of individuality, the situation could hardly be worse.

Sexual abuse can be physically painful, but it is more insidious when it is not. It is interesting that children, when lectured on molestation, are often told to report any touch from an adult that does not feel right. Without offering specificity, we somehow trust their intuitive judgment. Yet although the child knows that what is happening is wrong, there is often an autonomic element of sensual pleasure that confuses him, fostering the idea that perhaps he enjoys it, nay, even wants it, that his sexuality is questionable, and ultimately that he is responsible for the abuse, if it is abuse at all. Moreover, developing an association between the intuition that something is fundamentally wrong and the experience of sensual pleasure accompanying it is the obvious foundation for subsequent feelings of guilt and shame in relation to sensual or sexual stimulation, a syntax of experience that is not limited to molestation scenarios. Depending upon the degree of guilt and shame, the child-turned-adult may, to varying degrees, dissociate from his sexual and even sensual pleasure, holding it in contempt. In so doing, he not only is deprived of the personal growth and joy involved in a healthy, intimate relationship, but he attempts to preclude an integral piece of himself. When erotic and sensual arousal are suppressed, general affect tends to be muted as well, leaving him intellectually "top-heavy" and existentially lopsided. Warring within himself, there is little time or room for the process of outward volution. Most pointedly, the physical intrusion of sexual violation dehumanizes the child through objectification, not in the epistemological sense of the child being a finite object of knowledge, but in the sense of the child being an object like any other object, to be used for personal purposes without consideration of his subjectivity. This dehumanization is an act of total negation, robbing the child not only of the opportunity to individuate, but of his very ontological validity. Let us not forget the reactive rage and the devastating effects of its inevitable internalization, and again we paint a waking nightmare of conflict and subjugation.

The negation of individuality through the obscuration of organic form and the obstruction of its outward volution is the essence and foundation of peripheral being. Organic form tends toward its own outward volution, proceeding authentically from its center of being, not randomly, but in accordance with the seed of individuality that is given. Anything obstructing this process contributes to the spiritual and psychological death of the individual form. The child thus overlooked or overwritten is thwarted, lost in himself and in the world. Shrouded in self-anonymity, he is not driven by true desire and personal relevance, and therefore is never truly happy and fulfilled. He might, for example, become a lawyer, with other interests or none at all, because his father is a lawyer or otherwise wants this for him. Or he might "fall into" a vocational path for random or inconsequential reasons, such as convenience of travel, nepotism, or medical benefits. Despite any talent and success, his accomplishments represent existential stagnation, for they are inauthentic and proceed from the periphery of his being. For others, a gift can be a curse if there is no corresponding interest and passion. It is not uncommon for musical or intellectual prodigies to bear the burden of their talents or aptitudes by pursuing them vocationally when these talents are not the true sources of joy and fulfillment. They may receive endless accolades and achieve fame and wealth, and yet remain empty and despairing within. Relationships may be equally impoverished, due to the manifestations of the antidependent defense discussed above, or because of other poor object choices stemming from a deficient knowledge of one's true thoughts and feelings. It is quite common, for instance, for spouses to be selected for extrinsic reasons, to fulfill the standards and criteria of others. Such predilections are clearly not of the heart, and like one's vocational life, one's relational or personal life can also be devoid of meaning, riddled with the despair of pure form lacking substantive content.

Experientially unfamiliar with the principle of discovering freedom within structure, or liberating the spirit in the form, the individual remains spiritually obstructed, and the capacity for personal freedom and fulfillment is clipped. Alienated from his own being, spiritually impoverished, insecure and despairing, he is a creature of self-doubt and confusion, heavily infused with anxiety and depression. Every aspect of his being, spiritual, psychological, and physical, is in a state of disorder. Spiritually, he is dead, for even with a firmly held theism and the observance of a religious tradition, he does not feel spiritually alive. He does not awaken each day with a renewed vigor and lust for life, with an ever-rejuvenating liberated spirit that moves to love and perfect the finite order. Instead, the day may be dreaded, either vividly as such, or anesthetized as cynicism, and looked upon as meaningless routine with no personal significance and no escape, except perhaps for transient indulgences, vacations, and escapades that merely divert him from an unchanging backdrop. The passion for his work and relationships, the gratification of meaningful productivity and the joy of helping others to find the same, the self-knowledge and appreciation for the present moment, are all absent from his experience. Psychologically he is largely repressed, and often unclear about the reasons and motivations that compel his actions, a phenomenon that typically gets him into trouble. He is almost always his harshest critic, as his attention flitters nervously between himself and others in a social comparison process aimed at maintaining or regulating his fragile self-esteem. It is rare for him to be truly or completely satisfied with what he has or what he has accomplished, to "hit the high note," for the images of forsaken dreams always linger in the background of his awareness. For the most part he hungers for another life, a different time or place perhaps, or a getaway, a desert island, or an opportunity to sail into the sunset and never return. Or he might wish to be another person, or to have another chance at his own life. Physically, much of the time he is a silent, quaking mass of neuromuscular tension, adrenaline spikes, excess gastric secretions, and neurotransmitter imbalances. He tightens his muscles, taxes his heart, and burns holes in his stomach; from the standpoint of the inside of his body he could just as easily be staving off wild tigers.

Human disorder begins in and as the separative movement of love, moving against form in an act of subjugating and negating it. The separative movement is itself disorder, and as something cannot arise from nothing, disorder can only produce more disorder. The disorder thus produced is the state of being crushed and negated in one's individuality, of being frustrated and lost, deprived of the organic right to unfold. In this state there is little room in the emotional repertoire for much more than depression and anxiety. Indeed, depression and anxiety are the hallmark symptoms of human disorder, yet in considering them symptoms we must be circumspect in our analysis as to the actual locus of pathology. In other words, depression and anxiety are themselves not pathological, for they are appropriate given the existential situation in which they arise. Moreover, given the reification capacity of nomenclature and nosology, it is theoretically easy and immature to think of these emotions as disease entities in the individual. It would be more accurate to say that the individual is made to feel them, and that it makes as little sense to consider these emotional states pathological entities as it does to posit some neurological condition to account for the pain following a slap in the face. It is therefore a gross attributional error to suggest that the emotions are pathological, or that the person experiencing them is in some way sick or diseased. The locus of pathology lies solely and exclusively in the separative movement, which knows nothing of loving the finite order and cultivating it toward its proper perfection. Although the individual is naturally affected by the separative movement, to locate the pathology in her is to miss her, for her personality in its potential vastness and profundity is a considerably more comprehensive measure of her individuality than her emotional reactions to negation.

To avoid major and unnecessary theoretical and pragmatic complications, it is critical to underscore that the depression and anxiety we are considering are purely existential, or reactions to the cultural and familial subjugation of the individual. These reactive emotions are to be distinguished from the category of mood disorders that are genetically transmitted and principally grounded in hormonal irregularities and neurotransmission disturbances, colloquially referred to as "chemical imbalances." In the case of existential depression and anxiety, the importance of locating the pathology in the separative movement of disordered social interactions and not in the individual herself vindicates the individual. Focusing on appropriate reactions to pathogenic circumstances ignores the full depth and breadth of the individual's personality, as we seek to know and understand not her, but her "illness." Ascribing pathology to these reactions creates the impression that the individual and her emotions are sick, and must be "treated" accordingly. Her "disorder" is not that she is crushed from without, but is rather an internal disease entity that manifests as symptoms. The arts of diagnosing, treating, and (one hopes) curing the individual reinforce the illusion of her pathology, and deflect attention from the true pathogenic fact, which is the subjugation and negation of individual form.

Vindicating individuality means accepting it and allowing it to flourish. To say that the individual form is perfect unto itself, in its uniqueness, is to attest to the critical importance of accepting its uniqueness and not trying to change it. It is not to suggest that the form is without imperfections or pathology of its own, such as predispositions to certain physical and emotional diseases. Yet when the pathology of existential depression and anxiety is understood in the same way, as a disease entity in the individual, we become disease and symptom oriented, forgetting about the rest of the individual and the circumstances of the human condition that occlude the reality of her being. The individual in this situation is not sick and in need of being cured, but imprisoned and in need of liberation. It is the disordered social situation that needs to be cured, beginning with the recognition of the separative movement and its devastating effects, and the acknowledgment of its rootedness in a state of spiritual insecurity.

Shifting the locus of pathology from the individual to the situation vindicates the individual, but in no way relieves her of her imperfections. The seed of her being, in other words, is accepted as perfect *in its imperfection*, and there is absolute faith in the "correctness" of the natural movement of outward volution. Genetic predispositions notwithstanding, the individual has a psychological life as well as a physiological "inheritance," and to ground all physical and psychoemotional illness in a physicochemical substratum of DNA strands and environmental toxins renders consciousness and human experience inconsequential, which is the crassest epiphenomenalism. There is a world of thought, feeling, and sensation, of memory and anticipation, of relationship, of inspiration and drive to grow and to express, that contains its own pathogenic elements.

What, then, are these pathogenic elements? Whereas in terms of the physicochemical substratum the pathogens are "bad" genes and environmental toxins, in terms of the psychological or experiential substratum the pathogens are distorted, conflicted, and toxic thoughts, confused, conflicted, and unobjective feelings, physical and emotional pain, bad memories, and negative anticipations, all of which are constellated by an emotional nucleus of anxiety and depression. Like the pathogens of the physicochemical substratum, these psychological or experiential pathogens are manifested in both physical illness and psychoemotional illness. Somatically, the manifestations of "bad" psychology can range from skin conditions, muscle spasms and neuromuscular tension, and headaches and sinus problems to digestive and cardiovascular disease, asthma, and conversion disorders, all conditions that are said to be "psychosomatic," "psychophysiological," or "psychogenic." It is common knowledge that anxiety and depression attack the body in many ways, and that conflicted anger can lead to such phenomena as migraines and ulcers (Asaad 1996; Levenson 2006). Psychoemotionally, the manifestations of the nucleus of anxiety and depression are obvious, given the prevalence and variety of mood disorders principally characterized and categorized by these emotions. The widespread use of antidepressant and antianxiety medication underscores this fact. Nosologically speaking, there is going to be categorical variety, and variety within categories, as each situation is unique, characterized by a particular individual with a particular set of experiences. Within this body of individual experience, of problematic thought and feeling, physical and emotional pain, bad memories and negative prognostications, are the materials for unique configurations of disorder that particularize affective symptomotology by integrating it into individual profiles. These profiles may include cognitive and perceptual dysfunction, impairment of memory, fragmentation of experience and identity, and debilitated or underdeveloped intersubjective capacity in terms of communication, rapport, and empathy.

With little effort we can see that the psychological or experiential pathogens we have been discussing are the direct products of the separative movement. We have tried to show that the movement against form, in whatever fashion, acts to subjugate or negate form, in the case of human beings, by attacking the individual on the levels of thought, feeling, and sensation. The resultant distortion, conflict, toxicity, confusion, pain, anxiety, and depression shroud the individual in obscurity, and prevent or pervert a naturally occurring process of outward volution or individuation that is the foundation for spiritual and psychological fulfillment and happiness. Pathologizing the individual with disease entities is yet another form of subjugation and negation, for it still overlooks the individual. Focusing exclusively on symptoms is a form of sanctioned dehumanization, and is an iatrogenic process as well, for the more the symptoms are attended to, the more the individual is ignored. When individual form is not cultivated but obscured, individual being is predominantly peripheral. The only escape from this purgatory of existential inauthenticity is either divine intervention or psychotherapies aimed at uncovering the true self.

As the whole is always greater than the sum of its parts, a person must be viewed as more than a mere cluster of symptoms and maladaptive behaviors. This point underscores two fundamental approaches to the practice of psychotherapy. The first is the *symptom-focused* approach, which aims to assuage symptoms such as anxiety and depression, and to correct maladaptive behavior patterns. Any other aspect of one's personality and life not circumscribed by this intense focus is, for all practical purposes, irrelevant. The second is the *individuation* approach, which aims at the articulation and expression of one's true personality. The principle herein, which is our central thesis, is that human disorder results from obstructions to personal development, and that with flourishing individuality symptoms and disorder fall by the wayside like skin shed from a snake. Far from being irrelevant, the whole of one's personality is the very point of psychotherapy.

When we speak of articulating one's true personality we refer to a philosophy and a practice. The philosophical premise is that there is a true personality, both actually and potentially, and that it is as unique to the individual as a fingerprint or retinal scan. The practice is a psychotherapeutic art akin to sculpting in stone. Its work is not to mold, augment, embellish, or otherwise change the fundamental personality, but rather to reveal it as a sculptor reveals forms hidden in stone. As the sculptor reveals the form by a subtractive process of chiseling away that which is not the form, psychological sculpting reveals the true self by rendering transparent that which has obscured its recognition and thereby limited its development and expression. The individual coming for this psychotherapy is not understood to be defective and in need of repair, but imprisoned and in need of liberation.

The clinical application of psychological sculpting to peripheral being necessarily invokes, both theoretically and practically, the notion of consciousness and unconsciousness. Before attempting to articulate the art or process of sculpting, briefly revisiting this notion may help avoid some fundamental and consequential misunderstandings.

VII
Consciousness and Unconsciousness

If one were to witness a gory accident or otherwise horrific event, the immediate impulse would be to look away. Because the locus of the event is spatially definitive, to prevent further distress one may simply decide not to look back. In a similar way, when consciously entertaining an unpalatable thought, attention may be deflected and focused on something else. Yet since thought does not occupy space, it cannot be spatially definitive. How, then, is the thought kept from becoming conscious? How is it avoided? Moreover, how are thoughts that were never conscious kept from becoming conscious? It seems that somehow we must first know something in order to know that we do not wish to know it.

As the preeminent epistemological tool is the asking of a question, it is basic to metacognition that the way a question is framed both reveals its fundamental assumptions and shapes the directionality of thought. It is therefore crucial that we metacognize our questions to avoid becoming epistemologically skewed by our own presuppositions. As framed, the question, "How is thought kept from becoming conscious?" is replete with implied ontological categories and a general model of the human psyche that, for the most part, remain unobjectified and unchallenged.

The traditional and widely accepted model of psychological functioning rests on the assumption that consciousness is a special outgrowth of unconsciousness (Freud 1912, 1915b), which is yet another form of epiphenomenalism. We tend to think of consciousness as the surface of unconsciousness, as when we say that a thought or memory "rises to the surface of consciousness." That which rises to the surface necessarily comes from below, or from that which is topographically "*sub*conscious." The common usage of this term belies our fundamental characterization of unconsciousness as somehow beneath or "under" consciousness, ignoring that consciousness and unconsciousness, since they do not occupy space, cannot be spatially related. As pure metaphor, the topographical model of the human psyche is concretized, and unconsciousness is thus ascribed a status of primacy as the foundation or ground of consciousness. Evolutionarily it came first, and is therefore primal. It is the wide and deep sea of primordial darkness, and consciousness is but a film of sentience resting precariously on its surface. In its ultimate form of reification it is "the Unconscious," the fundamental principle or power of the human psyche. Revisiting the question of how a thought is "kept from becoming conscious," it is apparent that we see consciousness as a passive recipient of impressions determined by something other than itself. It is the last stage of registration in an otherwise unconscious world of censors, filters, repressive barriers, inhibiting ideas, microgenetic modes of information processing, and many other structures and functions that determine what should and should not be allowed to "enter" consciousness (Erdelyi and Goldberg 1977). In short, when a thought is kept from becoming conscious it is precluded by the dynamics of the Unconscious, which knows its contents, when they are tending toward "emergence," and how to counter this emergence by "pushing them back down." Hardly a fundamental principle or power in itself, consciousness is a mere determination of the Unconscious, both in its form and in its content.

We noted in the first chapter that finite consciousness must be grounded in infinite consciousness, which is the foundation of the universe and the very ground of Being. While containing or knowing time and space, infinite consciousness transcends time and space, and thus has no beginning and no end, both in time and in space. As the fundamental principle or power of the universe, it cannot be a mere surface or outgrowth of unconsciousness, or of anything else. Omnipotent by definition, it cannot be a relatively inert or passive receptacle for psychological data first processed and screened unconsciously, for then it is determined by something other than itself. And herein lies the problem. Consciousness and unconsciousness are not ontologically distinct. The implied principle in the traditional model that unconsciousness knows its contents leads to the consideration that perhaps the very term "unconscious" is unfortunate. To suggest that unconsciousness is the opposite or absence of consciousness implies some kind of void lacking in any content or form.

But unconsciousness is not the same as *no* consciousness. How else could it know its contents and process information intelligently? We discover that what we have been calling unconsciousness is actually consciousness itself, and thus we are compelled to construct an alternative model of the human psyche that posits consciousness as the fundamental principle or power of existence.

As already noted, we are accustomed to thinking of God the Infinite as omniscient as well as omnipotent; this should remove any difficulty in appreciating the fallacy of epiphenomenalism. If the Infinite is conscious, this is infinite consciousness. As a knowing Subject, undivided and outside time and space, infinite consciousness must know every finite object simultaneously and as immediately present to its entire Self. Moreover, it is in the nature of the Infinite, through the act of selfless love, to give or abandon itself to the finite, to assume finite points of view, or to know itself in time and space. This, too, should not be an unapproachable concept, given the commonplace theological distinction between the unmanifested God and his finite manifestations or creations. Finite consciousness, as a manifestation of infinite consciousness, is a particular point of view, or the span or field of sentience underlying the entire body of knowledge pertaining to a particular individual. By knowledge we do not mean the realm of ideas specifically, but all that is known to the individual, including feelings, sensations, perceptions, memories, and anticipations. What is typically deemed unconscious, whether incidentally, such as one's own name during an exciting sporting event, or purposefully, such as a repressed memory, is still known, and known, as it can only be, to consciousness. If that which is categorically unconscious is actually known to consciousness, we must then say that it is known in a different way than that which is conscious.

Consciousness, or the conscious Self, can know other things, but it cannot know itself, at least not in the same way. This is to say that consciousness cannot know itself objectively, or make itself the object of its own knowledge. The knowing subject and known object would be one and the same. In contrast to this objective and mediate knowledge, consciousness knows itself subjectively and immediately, in a manner that is as absolute and certain as the reality of one's being. The idea of the conscious Self knowing itself objectively is an artifact of language, for like light, the very fact of it being luminous obviates the need to illumine itself (Watts 1948).

The mode of knowing that we call subjective and immediate does not only pertain to the Self's knowledge of itself. The Self can know other things subjectively and immediately as well. They are still objects of knowledge, but *known* subjectively and immediately. To know something objectively and mediately is for the knowing Subject or conscious Self to distinguish itself from the known object. This is the simple fact of subject and object, self and other, here and there. Subjectively speaking, it is to know something from a distance. The closer the knowing subject is to the object, the harder it is to know it as such. It can be so close that the object, like a contact lens on the eye, is too close to be known or seen objectively. Yet we still know that it is there, as through mere surface contact the eye "knows" the presence of the lens, and that it is ontologically valid, as the lens is consequential when it cannot be seen. To know something as such is to know it subjectively, or what we typically call unconsciously. But unlike no consciousness, unconsciousness is actually quite conscious, though it knows its objects of knowledge without objectivity, like eye and lens. What we typically call consciousness is the same consciousness as unconsciousness, except that it knows its objects of knowledge objectively, or with psychological distance, distinguishing itself as such from the known object. Consciousness and unconsciousness are therefore not ontologically distinct, but rather two modes of knowing inherent to the conscious Self.

Most of what is known to consciousness is known subjectively. The mode of objective knowing, or the phenomenological eye, is but a small portion of the individual conscious field, much like central as opposed to peripheral vision, or a spotlight in relation to a floodlight. What we typically consider consciousness proper knows its objects of knowledge objectively, as they are thrown into stark relief, at a psychological distance from the knowing subject. Since it is in the nature of consciousness to give itself to the finite object, it cannot truly turn away or be deflected from it, for that which is selectively unconscious is actually known to consciousness, but in a different way. While the conscious Self cannot turn away from that which it knows and loves, it can certainly *zoom* in and out, knowing it from afar and then up close. It can be so close that the object becomes the background of one's awareness, no longer one of the objects in view. Still an object of knowledge, it is known subjectively or unconsciously.

That which is known objectively, or in the phenomenological eye, is highlighted by consciousness, or placed on center stage, in the spotlight.

It is clearly distinguished from other objects of knowledge, and from the knowing Subject. From the standpoint of consciousness, the ontological status of finite objects of knowledge does not vary with the mode in which they are known, that is, objectively or subjectively. To the psychophysical organism, however, that which is known objectively is the most compelling and vivid reality, or reality par excellence. In other words, that which lies in the conscious eye will have the most immediate and acute effect on the psychophysical organism, taken as the complex of thought, feeling, sensation, memory, and anticipation, or, in short, the ego. Moreover, the effect will be the same irrespective of the ontological status of the known object. A rapidly approaching tiger can be just as scary in a dream or hypnotic state as it can be in waking life. That anxiety-producing or otherwise unpalatable thoughts or ideas more acutely affect the psychophysical organism when known objectively mobilizes defensive measures to "repress" such mentation, which is actually not to bury or abandon it, but purposefully to know it subjectively. Unlike the eye turning away from a terrible scene, consciousness cannot turn away from that which it knows, but can bring it so closely into focus as no longer to know it objectively. As the foundation of existence and no mere determination of unconsciousness, consciousness transcends its objects of knowledge and is thus, in principle, infinite and omnipotent. As such, it retains the freedom to know the finite world objectively or subjectively. The question of how an unconscious idea is avoided or kept from becoming conscious is relevant only to the traditional and epiphenomenal model of human psychology. It would be more appropriate to ask why consciousness, *which always knows its objects,* moves to know certain objects in a subjective mode only.

VIII
Psychological Sculpting

Folklore has it that when Michelangelo was asked how he carved a figure as magnificent as the *David* from a block of stone, he replied, "I chiseled away everything that was *not* the *David*." In his sonnets he wrote of sculpting as the act of "liberating the figure imprisoned in the marble" (Nims 1998).

As a rule, all significant relationships are internalized, whether they are dialectical or didactic. With the internalization of a dialectical relationship the adult is introjected as a stimulant to ongoing dialectical processing, and because of these elements of freedom and individuality the internalized other is said to be integrated into the psyche of the child. With the internalization of a didactic relationship the adult is introjected as a hindrance to dialectical processing, and in the absence of freedom and individuality remains unintegrated in the psyche of the child. Looming as an officious and subordinating presence, the didactic introject, because never integrated into a dialectical relationship, remains an unchanged and autonomous entity, in the child but still foreign to his essential identity.

Ontologically speaking, the internalized dialectical process and the didactic instructiveness of the unintegrated introject are distinct in origin and nature. The thoughts that follow a dialectical process are clearly *of* the individual, and experienced in the first person as *my* thoughts. The thoughts that follow a didactic process are clearly of the other, and *should* be experienced in the first person as *his* or *her* thoughts. Simply because the didactic relationship has been internalized and the object representation is in the individual does not make it of the individual, any more than it was of the individual when purely embedded in the objective, preinternalized other. Internalization does not blur the ontological distinction between self and other, but unfortunately, with time, phenomenology does. What is originally his or her voice as an external facticity becomes, through memory, internally represented or "heard" as such in one's mind. As simple memory, the "voices" are clearly his or hers, and there is no confusion of identities. With ongoing repetition these *voice-memories* become less discernible as distinct characters, and seem to assimilate to oneself, so that we come to hear them in our own voice, as our thoughts. Although the ontological distinction between self and other is inviolable, consciousness is deceived into experiencing it otherwise, and therein is left open to boundless and devastating confusion.

Practically speaking, we may ask that if the didactic voices or thoughts are positive and benign, why should it matter that they are the voices of others camouflaged as our own? Why does this phenomenological distinction need to be made? This question amounts to asking why it is important to distinguish what is me from what is not me, or truly to know oneself. The didactic content may very well be positive and benign, but because it is communicated through a didactic process it is still subordinated to the larger didactic goal of negating the individual by precluding the element of dialectical freedom. The individual may have been "taught well," but to the degree that the element of freedom is absent, he is simply a victim of programming. Moreover, the didactic content is typically not positive and benign, especially when pertaining to the person of the child. The purpose of the didactic process is to impose social information on the child. To insure the efficacy of this process, the imposition of information must be in a fundamentally hostile medium. As an act of moving against form, the quest to teach a rapidly expanding mind *not* to think for itself requires force, or psychological bullying. Didactic content is thus replete with implicit and explicit injunctions, commands, admonitions, and threats. Moreover, didactic content, as part of a process of subjugation, also contains adult reflections of the child that tend to undervalue him, or distort his self-image into less than what he actually is. As the efficacy of the kill is augmented by the paralysis of the victim, how better to oppress than first to humble? It is thus intrinsic to the didactic process to create a measure of esteem deficiency in the child through distorted didactic content.

The process of thinking, as distinguished from imaging, involves, most specifically, the coexistence of the dialectical and didactic processes. Where the process of imaging, in its very definition, is the formation of

73

significant "visual" representations of the world, the process of thinking is the formation of significant "auditory" representations of the world. We speak, in this latter sense, of the inner *voice* or internal *dialogue*. We refer to thinking as self-*talk*, often substitute "I thought" with "I *said* to myself," and have such expressions as, "The music was so loud I could hardly *hear* myself think." The coexistence of the dialectical and didactic processes is one of complete incompatibility, tension, and conflict, for as the dialectical process tends toward its own ongoing freedom, the didactic process moves to restrict or prohibit this freedom. In a given individual, the respective strengths of these processes are reflected in respective degrees of open-mindedness, personal freedom, and individuality.

The dialectical process, in its essence, is an *open system*, for it is ever-flowing, changing, growing, and evolving. It is life, and it is health. The dialectical process *is* freedom, and grounded in this freedom is the capacity for self-knowledge and the outward volution of one's inmost and authentic being. That which manifests from the dialectical process, because it is grounded in freedom, is, ontologically, most definitively and absolutely oneself, or, in the first person, *me*. The didactic process, in turn, is a *closed system*, for it is static, unchanging, and exclusionary. It is death, and it is disease. The didactic process limits or prohibits freedom, and in so doing limits or prohibits the capacity for self-knowledge and individuation. That which manifests from the didactic process originates in the unintegrated but introjected didactic other, and because it is unintegrated into a dialectical process it is not grounded in freedom, and hence wholly other, or *not me*.

The importance of distinguishing what is me from what is not me is that it is the act of "liberating the figure imprisoned in the marble." When the process of individuation or outward volution is obstructed and subverted, the figure becomes hidden. The individual form is not cultivated but negated, and thus obscured and obstructed from expression. That which obscures and subjugates is the didactic process and its contents, assimilated to the voice of the individual, pulling him from his center of being to a necessarily false periphery. Distinguishing the didactic other, objectifying it and identifying it as such, is the sine qua non of releasing its hold on the dialectical freedom of the individual. As this hold is progressively released, the individual experiences a shift in his locus of identity from a false periphery to his true center of being, and that which had been obscured and smothered is gradually allowed articulation and expression.

The art of psychological sculpting, as a subtractive process of "chiseling away" that which is not the individual form, begins with the objectification of experience. The act of objectification is that of consciously *watching* finite objects of experience, whether "external," such as birds flying overhead and the passing of automobiles, or "internal," such as the flow of one's thoughts, feelings, and sensations. As we watch or objectify the process of thinking we are able to make some startling and important observations.

First and foremost, epiphenomenalism notwithstanding, we see that our thoughts are profoundly consequential in terms of influencing mood, self-concept and self-esteem, interpretive schemata, anticipatory disposition and general outlook, confidence and motivation, and behavior. Simple introspective study of the syntax of experience illustrates this obvious but profoundly important point. The thought "I will die one day" is certainly enough to attenuate a celebratory mood, as thinking "I'm stupid and ugly" will bear upon one's social and professional expectations and decisions. When these thoughts are conscious we do not always appreciate the causal link between thought and reaction, much less understand the origin or ontological status of the thought. When these thoughts are unconscious, this absence of raw phenomenological data leaves us only with effects, much like being smacked in the head by the Invisible Man. That which mediates such reactions as an unexplained shift in mood or unconscious motivation may be fleeting or otherwise indiscernible, but no less consequential. Since we cannot see the cause, we cannot establish it as the presyntactic moment to the effect, nor identify it for its origin and nature.

Second, through the process of objectification we are able to distinguish the dialectical and didactic processes. When a thought is objectified, not only can we appreciate its inestimable influence, but we can ask, "Whose voice is this?" When this question is posed to another person it typically elicits incredulous responses such as, "What are you saying, I'm schizophrenic?" Indeed it can be a disquieting question, but not simply because it involves misapplied diagnostic categories. It threatens the very integrity of one's psychic constitution, but the threat is not to the dialectical process. The didactic introject, as an unintegrated autonomous entity and insidious agent of control, must defend its dual agenda of programming the individual and making him think that it is his own control. To distinguish the dialectical and didactic processes is to identify the didactic process, to "blow its cover," to see it for *who* it really is. By identifying it as such, we disidentify with it, revisiting the primal ontological distinction between self and other. We realize that it is not me, that it is in me but not of me, much like a virus or any other foreign body invading the physical system. On physical grounds we intuit this principle when we excuse ourselves from a social invitation saying, "I'm sorry, but I have a raging head cold," and not, "I'm sorry, but I *am* a raging head cold." On psychological grounds this principle is thrown into stark relief when we recognize the didactic voice as his or hers, rendering it first visible by identifying it and then transparent by not allowing it to obscure the dialectical voice that is most definitely my own.

The very idea of disidentification with the didactic introject carries profound implications for the psychotherapeutic process. Most prominent is that the locus of pathology or disorder is not in oneself but in the other. The dialectical process is a manifestation of the principle of freedom, and is therefore not only the perfect illustration and symbol of individuation, but the very premise of mental health. As an open system, the dialectical process juxtaposes theses with antitheses, thus subjecting psychological toxins to scrutiny, and ultimately normalization through the resolution of the tension of triangulation. It is often said, in this regard, that mental health is the ability to consider alternatives. As a closed system, the didactic process is the premise of mental disease, for in form and in content it is designed to oppose the individuation process, and in its rigidity is resistant to alternative viewpoints and subsequent normalization. Establishing the locus of pathology in the introjected didactic other provides the esteem-deficient individual with much-needed validation and vindication, and mitigates resistance to the psychotherapeutic process. The embarrassment of being sick or deficient and in need of cure or repair is clipped from the equation, for it is no longer understood to be a matter of changing oneself, but rather freeing oneself from the effects of the didactic introject. The impossibility of a system changing itself, or trying to run from one's own shadow, is superseded by the viable task of achieving liberation from the oppressor.

Disidentification with the didactic introject also avoids the fatal misstatement of the psychological problem. When internal disparagement or so-called self-defeatism is viewed as a reflexive and monistic singular-pronoun scenario, the problem is erroneously framed and necessarily unsolvable. When hounded and tormented by the crippling reductionism of the toxic introject, the individual is often presented with the well-meaning but clumsy question, "Why do you do this to yourself?" The suggestion that it is a "self-on-self crime," that it is oneself disparaging and defeating oneself, generates a number of unnecessary complications. First, the individual is made to feel inadequate because she cannot answer a misstated question. Second, the implicit imperative that she stop this hounding creates agonizing exasperation and esteem-diminishing helplessness when she realizes that she cannot, not appreciating that she is placed in a double bind when compelled to stop doing something that she is not doing. Third, the individual is made to feel even more deficient and disordered than before, as it seems that it is she who is the abuser. Fourth, the individual is left defenseless against the toxic introject as her anger becomes self-directed, for after all, "she has no one to blame but herself."

Appreciating the syntax of experience in terms of the profound consequentiality of thought can be easy or difficult. The hypochondriac experiencing intense anxiety while sitting in her physician's examining room has no trouble identifying the presyntactic moment to this anxiety as thoughts anticipating a grave medical diagnosis. The thoughts are conscious, as is the relationship between these thoughts and the emotional reactions they mediate. In other instances this relationship is not so apparent. The nature of one's thoughts and the reverberations of these thoughts in the life of the individual are treated as isolated psychological "subsystems." The thoughts are conscious, as are the emotions, actions, and life situations they mediate. The element of unconsciousness is in the inability to appreciate the relationship between the two, thus rendering them isolated, at least phenomenologically. The dots are clearly visible, but there are no lines connecting them. As with isolated cognitive subsystems proper, such as contradictory viewpoints or philosophies *within* an individual, they are not juxtaposed or at once brought into view in order to examine the nature of their relationship. When contradictory viewpoints are examined closely for their relationship we discover one of mutual exclusivity. When the nature of one's thought is similarly juxtaposed to the actions and circumstances of one's life, we discover a mediational relationship in the sense that thought mediates, or carries with it, the potential for certain emotional reactions, judgments, and decisions that bear upon and shape one's life. We may loosely describe this relationship as "causal," but with reservations. Simple causality denotes a mechanistic construction of relationship, much like billiard balls or dominoes knocking into one another. The causative agent is not modified or transformed in the act of causation. As a mediational agent, thought is consistently modified by that which it mediates, characterizing the process as dialectical and not simply mechanistic. Moreover, the determinate nature of causation suggests that given a certain cause, a certain effect or effects must necessarily follow. That which is mediated by thought is probabilistically and not necessarily effected by thought, leaving room for the elements of freedom and overdeterminism.

It is often the case that an individual may be fully aware of and remember painful interpersonal experiences from childhood, and yet not connect them in any way to acknowledged problems with intimacy and relationship as an adult. Depending upon the degree to which the incognizance of this connection is incidental or purposeful, we encounter varying degrees of difficulty in helping to establish it. In the simplest case the connection was never made, and naivete or lack of sophistication is responsible for the overlooked syntax. We see this in the marked absence of resistance in the individual making this connection, grasping the relationship at once in a moment of revelation, intrigue, and surprise, often exclaiming, "Wow, I never thought of that." In other instances the syntax is harder to appreciate because efforts to articulate it are met with resistance. The element of relationship or connection is not simply unacknowledged but disacknowledged, repressed, or otherwise subjected to selective inattention. The attempt to overcome or dissolve this resistance then becomes the peremptory psychotherapeutic challenge.

Keeping with the distinction of moving with and moving against, we may approach this resistance in one of two ways. Analysis of resistance (Freud 1926), or a cogent intellectual construction of its nature, can be a powerful tool. As an act of moving against form, its movement is to break down or dissect resistance, and thus to see it for what it really is. It is not uncommon that an individual retains clear and conscious memories of verbal disparagement and physical abuse as a child, and is, at the same time, keenly aware that she has insecurities and could be doing more with her life. But to the incredulity and frustration of the therapist, she cannot see the relationship. From the therapist's standpoint the relationship is patently obvious, no less than the physical presence of the two individuals sitting in the room. How, in fact, could it be otherwise? Yet the individual sees no syntax. "That was then. This is now." "I don't like to blame things on the past." "I believe in taking responsibility for my life." Not alone in his incredulity, the therapist pushes the point. "But it's impossible for there *not* to be a relationship. Why is it so hard to acknowledge this?" The therapist is able to push the point and be confrontational, and this may continue over a period of time because he is not alone, because there is a piece of the individual that is allied with him and corroborates his position. If the individual believed the therapist to be completely skewed she would likely have discontinued after a few sessions. Persistent and to the point, but absolutely benign and with the weight of shared incredulity behind him, the therapist gently prods and encourages the individual to engage in dialectical exchange, at least to speculate, to free her mind to possibility. And then, with either reflective consternation or idle flippancy, a pearl of information is yielded, with the individual declaring something like, "I'd hate to think that my parents still have such influence over me," or, "It's hard to think of them as capable of so much damage." With these golden keys we are able to help the individual realize that she is resisting what she already knows, that her abusive past has been holding her down, and that true assumption of responsibility is the acceptance of this reality, for it is the starting point of an unimagined and unprecedented existential freedom.

The complementary approach to dealing with resistance is to move with it, or to *join* it (Spotnitz 1985). To move with the form of resistance is not to controvert its premise, but rather to act consistently on it. To the person blindly maintaining the position that the earth is flat we give a boat and a cell phone, and ask him to call us the moment he tips over the edge. Likewise, if it is true that present fears and inhibitions are not mediated by particular abusive others, past and present, what then is their origin? *Ex nihilo nihil fit.* Something cannot come from nothing. Did God do this to the individual? Or did the individual do it to himself? Did the individual make himself fearful and self-doubting? And if so, why? Would he not have to be astronomically stupid or mentally diseased to choose this course when there were so many others at his disposal? It makes no sense. As the fool who persists in his folly becomes wise, the path of least resistance helps us see the error of false assumptions. Of course it is the abusive others who injure us, who set limitations in our lives. Yet as we ardently fight to deny this we cannot see that it is actually the act of accepting it that eventually sets us free, for in so doing we identify the toxic factor as the other, as not me, and thereby set the stage for self-discovery, growth, and expression, which is the ultimate instance of taking responsibility for one's life and being.

In other instances it is not the incognizance of relationship between thought and that which thought mediates that diminishes appreciation for the consequentiality of thought. It is the incognizance of the very thought or idea itself. When we speak of unexplained mood shifts or unconscious motivation, for example, we speak only of effects, with the mediational events not in the phenomenological eye. So often it happens that one's mood will suddenly change for no apparent reason, or that one will engage in a self-destructive act without understanding why. In lieu of careful psychological inquiry it is all too easy to attribute such phenomena to "chemical imbalances." This is not to suggest that the chemical imbalance is a mythical construct, but rather that it is overused in the service of intellectual corner-cutting. With due diligence and determination we may be surprised by the availability of discernible psychological mediators that account for otherwise unexplainable phenomena. As with the incognizance of relationship between conscious thoughts and effects, the fact of these mediators being *un*discerned may either be incidental or purposeful.

In the simplest case we begin with the consideration that thought, whether didactic or dialectical, is both fleeting and multitudinous, and that like lightning flashing through the mind, it can easily go unnoticed. When a thought of significant consequence is incidentally unconscious it is simply not noticed, or what Freud (1933) called *preconscious*. Through a simple act of selective attention deployment it is conscious readily enough, such that, when so instructed, the individual can isolate it, either by catching it in the moment or retrieving it after the fact. The therapist may say something like, "I noticed that your mood just changed. What are you thinking?" Or retroactively he may ask, "Last night when you became anxious, what were you thinking?" Quite surprisingly, we discover that more often than not, when directed in this way, the individual is able to isolate or identify relevant mentation, and ultimately appreciate the syntactical relationship between thought and that which thought mediates. It is important to note, in this regard, that mentation is *always* ontologically valid in that it is of actual or potential consequence (Bowers 1984; Erdelyi 1985; Erdelyi and Goldberg 1977; Silverman 1983). Its phenomenological status, however, is a function of whether it is in the eye of consciousness, or whether it has been distinguished from the knowing subject by becoming an object of knowledge. If it is not distinguished as such, it is phenomenologically nonexistent, or unconscious, but no less valid ontologically. Its very nature and the fact of its consequentiality, in other words, are certainly not negated by being outside the scope of awareness. We see this principle clearly exemplified in instances when sustained and focused attention on an unsolved problem is temporarily relinquished due to either exasperation or fatigue. The despairing intellect may allow itself to think of other things, wander aimlessly, or contemplate the stars, when suddenly, without notice, the solution "pops" into one's mind. It is clear that when the light of consciousness was deflected from the process of thought, the process continued, in much the same way that we do not fall from bed at night as we reconnoiter its edges even while asleep. Isolating a mediating thought, or bringing in into the phenomenological eye, illuminates the presyntactic moment to a problematic reaction, and creates the first tier of leverage against its destructive influence. Speaking in the first person, by silhouetting the Invisible Man with spray paint, I can now see what is smacking me in the head, and thus be better positioned to protect myself from it.

When a thought of significant consequence is purposefully unconscious, the principle of repression is invoked (Freud 1915a). Isolating or identifying relevant mentation, in this instance, is met with considerable resistance, and is not a matter of a simple attentional shift. There is a movement against the objectification of the thought that is in the service of a psychological defense. A severely depressed young mother may experience concomitant anxiety reactions that can easily be attributable or "secondary" to her depression. It is conceivable, however, that her mind entertains a passing fantasy of smothering her infant, and that this is the source of her anxiety. Given the absolute and mortal transgression of such an idea, there is a movement against it being objectified or conscious, while it is still ontologically valid as it continues to mediate anxiety reactions. As before, we may either move with the resistance or move against it. When moving with it, we accept the movement against objectification and the void that it creates. Instead, we pay careful attention to that which outlines the void, like bricks outlining a window. Thoughts, feelings, memories, fantasies, fears, and the like continue to constellate around the repressed idea, and an entire complex or chain of associations typically cannot be blotted from consciousness. As the bricks shape the window, the rich associative activity surrounding the repressed idea helps define it. Our depressed and anxious young mother, for example, may develop paranoid fears of somebody else hurting her child, and ultimately construct compulsive rituals of frequently checking on the child to allay her concerns. Unfortunately, not all situations are so readily accessible to inferential thinking, but the point is that context can be used to carve semantic inroads into a phenomenological void.

When moving against the resistance we analyze it. We precisely do not accept the movement against objectification, but rather seek to understand, confront, and challenge it so that it may be undermined. An individual not wishing to discuss a particular topic may be willing to talk about why she does not wish to discuss it. Similarly, an individual not wishing to think or be aware of a particular thought may be encouraged to explore the difficulty involved in addressing the issue. When asked why she believes she's fearful in the absence of any empirical threat, the young mother in our example may become defensively unreflective, and quick to dismiss the question with a precipitous "I don't know." With gentle persistence the therapist may then point to her obvious discomfort and help describe and identify it. "You seem uncomfortable with this line of questioning. What's the feeling?" Depending on the woman's introspective capacity and level of resistance to therapy, the quest to isolate her emotional discomfort will vary in difficulty. If the therapist can elicit a substantive response, the delineated negative affect may be used in two ways. First, if the discomfort can be allayed, we begin to mitigate the movement against the objectification of the repressed idea. Second, the nature of the discomfort, as one aspect of the associative activity surrounding the repressed idea, can help define it. If, for instance, the woman reports feelings of anxiety and guilt, the therapist may attempt to allay this guilt by consistently reminding her that thoughts qua thoughts are just thoughts, and that in the realm of silent interiority morality is inapplicable, since pure mentation cannot hurt anyone. Moreover, the therapist may question the significance of the guilt, or how a measure of personal responsibility bears on the interpretation of a paranoid fear. Moving against or analyzing the resistance as such can effectively attenuate it, and help discern contextual clues about the nature of the repressed idea. Either way, we again meet the objective of carving semantic inroads into a phenomenological void.

With clear consciousness of the syntax of experience, or the relationship between thought and what it mediates, the individual can appreciate, in terms of inner dialogue, what is being "said" and how it affects him, for thought is always ontologically valid in that it is of actual or potential consequence. Unlike "simply" being in a bad mood or "inexplicably" committing a self-defeating act, the presyntactic moment to the problematic reaction is objectively known. The individual is in a bad mood because he is facing a new challenge and feels inadequate and fearful of failure. "I'm basically an idiot who can't do anything right." He defeats himself by avoiding the challenge and preempting the inevitable. "Better I should quit than be fired." With this awareness he now knows what is affecting him problematically and how.

But this is not enough. How does he protect himself from such toxic declarations? At whom should he be angry for this internal abuse? Does he not do this to himself? He must, since he thinks, "*I'm* an idiot who can't do anything right." Clearly it is the individual talking to himself. Any angry criticism for having these thoughts must then be self-directed, and thus he is thrown into the impossible bind of the individual ego leveraging against and changing itself. But if he consistently objectifies and "listens" to what is being said, he may notice that it is really not "I'm an idiot," but rather, "*You're* an idiot." He may discover, in other words, that the situation is not reflexive but social, and that it is the other who is talking to him. Asking "Whose voice is this?" is pointing not to schizophrenia, but to the unintegrated didactic introject that has been hiding behind his own voice. Has the abusive other not said this to him many times in the past, either explicitly or implicitly? Can he not hear it in his voice or hers, or even bring it back to specific instances in memory? By identifying what is being said and *who* is saying it, the individual clearly discerns the didactic introject as the other, as in him but not of him, and thereby disidentifies with it. As such, he is now sufficiently leveraged to protect and free himself from its effects.

Having rendered the didactic process visible by identifying what and who it is, psychological sculpting can now move to render it transparent by releasing its hold on the dialectical process. Releasing the dialectical process from the crippling grip of the didactic introject is no easy task. Next to confronting one's own mortality or that of a loved one, it is perhaps the greatest human challenge. Sadly, the ultimate indomitability of the human spirit is rarely given expression, as most people never even identify this challenge, much less meet and accomplish it. The disastrous results of this psychological imprisonment are seen in the pervasive and chronic disruption of human relationships. Marriages are typically unsuccessful and replete with misery. Employee dissatisfaction is the norm, as corporate relations and management skills are clearly substandard. Family gatherings for holidays and other celebrations may be benign in principle, but are typically fraught with acute self-consciousness and simmering resentments that lead to an impatient eye on the clock and a knotted stomach awaiting antacids. Friendships and allegiances are unnecessarily complicated and constantly shifting, and wherever there is some kind of divide, contention exists. Our technology has so far surpassed our socioemotional maturity that we are but children possessing twenty-first-century weaponry. When the process of individuation is clipped from the human experience, and the individual is dominated by the didactic introject, it is impossible to negotiate objective and uncomplicated relationships. Even as two people meet de novo, their respective microcosms of internal disorder will largely configure the macrocosm of their interaction and relationship. Despite the passage of time and the physical absence of historical figures, they remain embroiled in their own netherworlds of shadowy objects or objective relations shrouded and contaminated by the internalized politics of the family.

Consistent with the themes we have been developing, attenuating the powerful hold of the objectified didactic introject may be accomplished by moving with it or against it. To move against the introject is to renounce and denounce it. It is in the nature of human emotion for pain to lead to rage, or hurt to anger. When unconflicted, this anger follows its natural course, which is to mobilize the individual to defend himself from the source of pain. This angry defense is not passive or principled, and it does not move to resolve conflict or understand the perspective of the hostile source. It is definitive and absolute, and it moves to annihilate or negate the didactic introject instead of letting the introject negate the individual. The didactic content, or what is being said, is irrelevant and unaddressed. Rather, it is the introject itself that is scrutinized, for in intrapsychic terms, angry renunciation manifests as countercriticism and devaluation, or the psychotherapeutic equivalent of discrediting the witness. To be able to turn to the abusive internalized father, for example, and with utter sincerity, congruence, and conviction say something like, "You only disparage me because of the way you were disparaged," or "You fill me with fear because of your own insecurities," is a pathway to liberation. The act of discreditation renders the didactic introject impotent by destroying its credibility, much like discovering that an astute and compelling psychiatric evaluation was written by Charles Manson. In so doing, the individual creates the freedom to think for himself, or liberate the dialectical process. Special emphasis must be given to the fact that countercritical declarations such as those mentioned are completely powerless if rendered as empty superficialities stated in a rote and repetitive manner. Like the unconvincing and stilted cadence of daily affirmations or positive "self-talk," mechanically uttered vindicating declarations that ring of "cold" anger are vapid and impotent. For countercriticism to be effectively discrediting it must be fueled with the fire of angry renunciation.

It is important to remember that dialectical liberation through congruent countercriticism of the didactic other necessarily pertains to the realm of internal object relations. Angry devaluation of the external object can be a fruitless endeavor, for it typically meets with angry defensiveness and counteraccusations of persecution designed to make the accuser feel guilty and deficient. Even if the external object assumes responsibility and is sincerely remorseful, there is still the problem of the introject, which is unaffected by the redemption of its external counterpart. Since the introject functions as an autonomous entity, unintegrated into the psyche of the individual, it functions on its own terms. It has its own motivations and modi operandi, as if it were the external object itself. When facing discreditation, it will therefore move to defend itself in the manner of the external object. If critically confronted with accusations of mistreatment or abuse, the external object will typically defend itself by using one or a combination of three strategies. Each strategy is an assaultive double entendre, as it explicitly denies responsibility for the abuse, while implicitly or subtextually pathologizing the individual for the very accusation. When confronting the introject, one or more of these strategies will likely manifest, and the individual must be prepared to deal with them. In the first instance the introject categorically denies the abuse ("That never happened," "I never said that"), with the implication that the individual is crazy. In the second instance the introject affirms the abuse, but blames it on the individual ("You made me do it," "You left me with no choice"), with the implication that the individual is bad. In the third instance the introject affirms the abuse, but mitigates the severity ("It wasn't nearly so bad as you describe it"), with the implication that the individual is too sensitive.

The danger of the outrageous declaration lies in the tendency of the recipient to corroborate it. This tendency is twofold in origin. First, there is a vulnerable core in each of us that lends us to self-doubt. Second, since much of what we call reality is consensually validated, sanity and consciousness are easily susceptible to social pressure (Asch 1951; Berger and Luckmann 1966). The moment angry renunciation and criticism of the didactic introject are met with denial, counterblame, or accusations of hypersensitivity is the moment of truth. If any of these strategies is corroborated, the individual is jettisoned into the vicious cycle of directing angry criticism toward himself, and thus protecting and sustaining the introject. In the prototypical example, the individual moves to vindicate himself by declaring, "I always thought I was bad, but *you* were abusive. I was a good kid." Typically defensive and deflective of responsibility, the introject replies, "You're making too much of it. You've always overreacted to things." And then, with the indignity of compelled self-effacement, the individual corroborates. "It's true. I do over-react. I shouldn't be angry at him." In this moment of corroboration the hypnosis has been induced and the lethal blow has been struck.

If one is ever to find freedom through individuation, the time must come to stand up to psychological bullying. Since the likelihood of internal corroboration or self-doubt is a given, it is critical to be keenly aware of it, to watch it ever so intently and not try to repress it. By watching it we keep it objectified, and by keeping it objectified we see it for what it is, and in its larger context. We are aware of the corroboration, and that it is an act of submission to the will of the subjugating other. When it is patently clear that our minds are being manipulated and turned against us in this act of subjugation, we become angry and defensive, and necessarily so. Once again there is a movement to strike against the introject, to renounce it through discreditation, to see through it and divest it of its hypnotic power by objectifying its motives and means. As the curtain is pulled aside, the great and powerful wizard is exposed. Behind the intimidating visage of thunderous credibility lurks a small and insecure figure, pulling levers and blowing smoke to restitute his own damaged soul through the subjugation of the other. Seen in perspective, he becomes transparent, and as his power dissipates so does the meaningfulness of his words.

To move with the didactic introject is to accept it, not in the sense of passive submission, but by bringing it into dialectical discourse. It cannot be emphasized strongly enough that the dialectical process represents the principles of life and health, and that, as an open system, it moves to normalize skewed ideas through the juxtaposition of alternative viewpoints. The didactic content, in this instance, is not discounted in an act of angry renunciation, but carefully considered through a process of intellectual triangulation. It is often said, in this regard, that sunlight is an excellent sanitizer, and accordingly, wresting a distorted proposition from the dark corner of intellectual isolation exposes it to the light of dialectical freedom and truth.

The power of the introject is never absolute, for there is always an element of dialectical processing, even under the dominion of the most aggressive didactics. The therapist's job is to tap this processing by encouraging and stimulating the individual to think divergently, or dare to question what he has been taught. It is an act of facilitating dialectical thought, and allowing it to perspectivize and incorporate didactic pathogens. As these pathogens are assimilated by the dialectical process, their toxicity dissolves through the necessary normalization that comes from saturating a skewed idea with multiple, alternative perspectives. Conversely, it is for the same reason that loss of sanity can result from solitary confinement or other forms of social isolation. What might otherwise pass for "knowledge," "reality," and "truth" are seen to be malignant lies and distortions aimed at oppressing or limiting individual growth and expression. The inestimable existential pain and stagnation wrought by didactically derived propositions such as "I'm not good at anything" or "Life is an exercise in futility" are sustained as long as these propositions are not scrutinously questioned. When illuminated by multiperspectival intellectual examination ("Is it true that I'm not good at anything?" "Is life really futile?"), falsehoods and distortions are exposed as diaphanous specters bereft of validity. Like osteoporotic bone, these didactic pathogens crumble, and as they are blown away by the wind, thought patterns normalize and the foundation for existential freedom is established.

We have described psychological sculpting as consisting of two processes: the objectification and identification of the didactic introject, and the release of the constricting hold of this introject on dialectical thought. We may just as easily describe this as a single, unitary process, or a complex integration of multiple processes. The point is that, as a therapeutic technique, psychological sculpting is effective when it renders the didactic introject visible, and then transparent. The didactic process moves to negate the individual by precluding the element of dialectical freedom. In the absence of this freedom there is no individuation, no outward volution, no true discovery, growth, and expression. The organicity of life is obstructed and subverted as the individual is insidiously peripheralized, or pulled from his center of being. Progressively deprived of any opportunity for passion and meaning, his life becomes psychologically and spiritually bereft. Divesting the introject of its power and thereby lifting its oppressive influence is thus the essence of effective psychotherapy and the surest path to salvation.

IX

The Spirit in the Seed

Unum quodque tendens in suam perfectionem tendit in divinam similitudinem.
"Whatever tends to its own perfection tends to a divine likeness." Despite
the limitations of language, in this one simple declaration Saint Thomas
Aquinas purely and directly touches upon the ultimate meaning and
purpose of life. For Saint Thomas it is not a matter of tending toward the
perfection of Jesus, God, Buddha, or anyone else. It is tending toward
one's own perfection, one's own individuation, and in so doing tending to
a divine likeness. In religious language, a divine likeness is not being like
God. It is being what God created. It is being oneself, in one's given nature,
created as such by God. To thine own self be true. If we are to speak at
all of a destiny, it is not in the Calvinistic sense of predestined actions and
events. It is in the fact that an individual form has a given nature, and that
under proper conditions this natural configuration unfolds, in its own way,
along its own lines and on its own terms. Even as two gametes meet, the
spirit is in the seed, and the free movement of the spirit is in the outward
volution of the individual form, proceeding authentically from its center
of being. If this cultivation of individuality is ongoing, if it is a way of life,
then there is no fundamental distinction between the spiritual life and
everyday life. "So long as man identifies himself with the ego he is trying to
be God. It is only when he knows that the center of his being is the infinite
that he is really free to be man, for we have seen that it is in the very nature
of the infinite to accept, include and abandon itself to the finite. This is
why the most spiritual people are the most human people. They are natural
and easy in manner; they give themselves no airs; they interest themselves

in ordinary everyday matters, and are not forever talking and thinking *about* religion. For them there is no difference between spirituality and usual life, and to their awakened insight the lives of the most humdrum and earth-bound people are as much in harmony with the infinite as their own" (Watts 1948,128). The spirit is not sought *up* or *out* there, or some time in the future, as something that is isolated from the finite world because of its transcendence. The spiritual life is nowhere but here and now, expressed as the unitive movement of love, moving with form in its ongoing articulation and expression.

We spoke earlier of religious institutions, of the double-edged sword of religion, and of the unfortunate rift between religious precept and religious character. Though suffering its own limitations, religion is necessary, and fundamentally good. It is what people do to it and with it that vitiates its purity of intent. Bigots and cowards hide behind it. The emotionally insecure use it to uplift themselves through an act of spiritual one-upmanship. The spiritually insecure look to rigidify it in their insatiable quest for reification. The personally unfulfilled use it to justify their frustration and unhappiness. Schizophrenics can get lost in it, and megalomaniacs desecrate it by using avowed deference to God to try to become God. The hypocrisy and politics of religion as it has been practiced have spawned many a wayward soul, but not without a certain need. We hear many people say, "I'm not religious, but I'm a very spiritual person." Typically this means that the person believes in a "higher" power, in karma, reincarnation, a moral code, or the conviction that there is meaning and purpose to life, and that there is some integral order to the universe. Sometimes this scope is widened to include belief in angels, ghosts, spirits, and other forms of so-called paranormal phenomena. The need that has been unfulfilled by the disappointment and failure of religion persists, for the individual is still driven by the desire to be connected to something greater than himself. The danger with such forms of spirituality is that they often harden into systems of fanciful beliefs and ideas married to strong sentimentality and emotion, with the individual still not experiencing the freedom and happiness of outward volution and personal growth.

Despite its miraculous achievements, science does not quench the spiritual thirst because its fundamental objective is mastery over nature. Necessary and integral to human life though it may be, its operant premise is not to cultivate but to control. When man seeks affinity or oneness with God by questing to contain his omnipotence, he not only attempts the impossible, but reinforces the very feeling of isolation and finitude that drives him to do this.

When religion as practiced and sundry spiritual ways and beliefs offer no relief from the existential angst of isolation and tentativeness, our quest for affinity with that which is greater than ourselves persists. We join organizations, ally ourselves with causes and movements, become devotees of people and principles, and even commit suicide. Yet we fail to see that the very fact of the quest reveals and reinforces the feeling of isolation and finitude.

The profound need to unite with something greater than oneself overlooks the reality that one already is, and has always been, that which is greater; that his consciousness is, in principle, one with the Infinite consciousness. When this is a realization and not simply a concept, the insecure hunger for God as an object disappears, and is replaced by a spiritual security that is replete and overflowing, selflessly lending itself to the perfection of the finite order. The conscious Self or Spirit, in other words, moves with form in an act of cultivation. Being infinite, it needs no objects. Abandoning itself thus, it knows and creates its objects, the finite world, and loves them accordingly (Watts 1948). Loving them selflessly, it develops them in accordance with their limitations. Cultivating individuality of form - in this instance, personality and character - is the essence of the spiritual life, for all of its expansive freedom, fulfillment, selflessness, and joy. Tending to a divine likeness is not man as man trying to be or possess God. It is man *as God* manifesting himself as man, in his fullest individuality.

Depending upon its anthropological assumptions, theoretical premises, practical applications, and objectives, the practice of psychotherapy, along with artful child rearing, may well be the second secular vehicle for spiritual liberation. Since its forms are manifold, we must examine them categorically to understand their relevance to what we consider the ultimate psychotherapeutic objective.

Psychoanalysis and psychoanalytic psychotherapies are founded on the anthropological assumption that man is fundamentally a "seething cauldron" of impulses and appetites that blindly press toward immediate gratification, and that must be restrained and sublimated lest he slip into individual and social chaos (Freud 1923). So invoked is the image of the angel riding the wild horse. The bucking bronco is, of course, the id, which knows no principle other than tension reduction or entropy. The controlling angel is the ego and superego, in part socially constituted, in part engendered by the need for mediation between instinctual demands and the limitations of external reality. The objective of psychoanalysis and psychoanalytic therapies is principally to "make the unconscious conscious," to understand current feelings and motivations vis-à-vis past experiences, and ultimately to establish objective and uncomplicated object relations in personal and professional settings. Psychological and emotional health depends on the ability of the ego and superego to tame the vast and dark atavistic Unconscious, redirecting it into socially constructive discourse. Civilization and order are nothing more than controlled chaos, and we must forever guard against and mistrust our ontological core.

Cognitive and cognitive-behavioral therapies (Beck 1976) are founded on the assumption that man is principally a creature of reason and intellect, invoking the Cartesian formulation *cogito ergo sum*. Psychological and emotional disorders are the result of maladaptive thought patterns, assumptions, and beliefs that produce depression and anxiety, self-defeating actions, and disruptions in human relationships. The objective of cognitive therapies is to correct maladaptive thinking, not by liberating the dialectical process and its movement toward normalization, but through the modification of thought qua thought. Psychological and emotional health rests on realistic and facilitating thoughts and thought patterns that regulate mood, inspire productive and adaptive behavior, and negotiate satisfying and rewarding relationships.

Behavioral therapies (Dollard and Miller 1950; Lazarus 1971), view man as an integrated system of response patterns that can be selectively reinforced, modified, or extinguished depending on the presence of specific environmental contingencies. Unencumbered by abstract notions such as mind, subjective experience, personality, and character, behaviorism as a philosophy values only that which can be observed and measured. The objective of these therapies is to condition or modify behavior, with the salubrious intent of producing a well-functioning and socially adapted human being.

Interpersonal therapies (Sullivan 1953) view man as preeminently a social being, *homo socius,* whose very nature, experience, and activity cannot meaningfully be understood outside the context of his social interactions. With genuine use of his own personality in forming a relationship, albeit professional, with the client, and through study of this relationship as well as the client's relationships with others, the therapist can help identify and improve deficits in communications and other interpersonal skills. The goal of successful therapy and the measure of mental health are in terms of the individual's capacity for facilitative and enriching relationships with others.

Jungian psychotherapy and its school of analytic psychology (Jung 1928, 1934) view man as both a personal and a *transpersonal* being, as individual and manifest, and as transcending the individual order. As the "seat of consciousness," the ego is positioned in relation to the personal unconscious and the collective unconscious. The personal unconscious is essentially Freud's unconscious, consisting of the individual's drives, impulses, and repressed thoughts, emotions, and memories. The collective unconscious consists of the archetypes, which, by definition, transcend the individual order as forms, and yet manifest in this order as content. This is to say that the archetype per se can never be an object of knowledge. It can only be known indirectly or symbolically as it manifests itself in human consciousness and culture. The supraordinate archetype is the Self, at once the center and "circumference" of the psyche, the organizing principle of psychic life, the symbol of wholeness, balance, and integration. The Self is the inmost seed of human being, and it moves toward outward volution. The objective of psychotherapy with relation to the personal unconscious is essentially the Freudian objective, but without the unique emphasis on the centrality of the Oedipus complex. With relation to the collective unconscious, the objective of therapy is for the ego to progressively integrate the contents of the collective unconscious and thereby establish an axis of balance between the ego and the Self. In Jungian terms, the assessment of mental health is relative to phase of life. The "first half" of life, for instance, is fundamentally extraverted, and oriented toward laying foundations and stability for family and career, for love and for work. Health and adaptation are understood in terms of the success of these endeavors. The "second half" of life is fundamentally introverted, and oriented toward self-discovery and personal growth. Psychological and emotional well-being are predicated on this outward volution *as an ongoing process*, for the Self, in essence ineffable, can never be fully actualized.

Client-centered or nondirective therapy originated in the humanist movement of psychology, as represented most notably by Carl Rogers (1951) and Abraham Maslow (1954, 1962). From this standpoint, man is essentially a self-actualizing being, replete with talents, capacities, and potential. As part of a more general organismic movement toward higher levels of health, creative expression, and insight, this inherent potential calls for a full and joyous use and exploitation. Neurosis or psychological disorder in its various forms is a by-product of the blockage or obstruction of this innate tendency toward self-actualization. The objective of client-centered therapy is to use supportive but nondirective discourse to help the individual, in the push toward personal growth and knowledge, gain a better sense of self and become more self-reliant.

We have been trying to show that, far from being an epiphenomenon of neurochemical activity, consciousness is infinite in principle, and thereby the very ground of the finite universe. Because it is infinite, it gives, abandons, or surrenders itself to the finite world in an act of selfless love. By loving and accepting the limitations of the finite order, the Infinite knows it and brings it into being. Spirit creates form in the act of knowing it. As two gametes unite, a new form is created, both *in actu* and *in potentia*, and its inherent movement is to unfold biologically and psychologically. From its inception the spirit is in the seed, and the free movement of the spirit is in the outward volution of the individual form, proceeding authentically from its center of being. Naturally and optimally this outward volution calls for social facilitation, or the selfless love of others that tends to the cultivation of form. The inverse of social facilitation is the obstruction and subversion of the outward volution of personality. Form is subjugated as the didactic process moves to negate the individual by precluding the element of dialectical freedom. Not only is the outward volution of personality obstructed, but so is the very movement of the spirit, for when the individual is peripheralized his life is necessarily robbed of passion and meaning.

It might be overstating the point to underscore the artificiality of the distinction between the psychological and the spiritual, for indeed, the very terms "psyche" and "spirit" share an etymological root. Yet functionally speaking we are compelled to act as if the distinction is real, depending upon our understanding of the nature of man and the consequent scope of the psychotherapy undertaken.

When we consider the various psychotherapeutic approaches together we discern two operant metaphors regarding the nature of man: *man as mechanism* and *man as organism*. The mechanical metaphor has man as a machine, both physically and mentally. He is viewed as an assemblage of parts and functions that are harmonious and coordinated when he is in a state of ease, and disharmonious and uncoordinated when he is *dis*eased. The organic metaphor has man as a process of outward volution and differentiation, like a germinating seed. He is understood not as an assemblage, but as a system of functions and structures that grow from within out. Disease and disorder result when this growth is obstructed.

The cognitive, behavioral, and hybrid cognitive-behavioral approaches to therapy proceed from the metaphor of man as mechanism. Maladaptive thought and behavior are to be modified mechanically, from without, as thought and behavior qua thought and behavior. The individual may be "liberated" from the restraints of bad learning and conditioning through modification or replacement of one set of cognitive-behavioral structures with another, but not necessarily through liberation of the dialectical process per se. Despite its heavy biological infusion, psychoanalysis is predominantly mechanistic as well. Freud's psychology, as it has been argued, bears remarkable similarities to contemporary cognitive theory, with points of disparity resting primarily on terms and metaphors and not concepts (Erdelyi and Goldberg 1977). Moreover, the substratum of Freud's biological organism consists of drives, which are fundamentally blind and peremptory, and in themselves illustrative of pure selfishness and anarchy. The organism is not thought to be intelligent, but chaotic and in need of control. The interesting irony is that the "higher" controlling agencies, the ego and superego, are configured of thoughts, feelings, sensations, and judgments that would have to be manifestations of the same blind and stupid organicity that manifests our rage and basic appetites. In accepting this principle we revert to the absurd reductionism of something coming from nothing. The essential definition of man as organism implies *intelligent* organicity, manifested as a process of unfolding and individuation.

The interpersonal, Jungian, and humanistic approaches to therapy hold to a more organismic view of man. The very premise of interpersonal philosophy is the development not simply of facile relationships, but of relationships of increasing intimacy as well, which is necessarily a process of ongoing discovery and growth. Jung's therapeutic goal of individuation, which is the movement of the archetypal Self as the center of being, is likewise an intelligent process of outward volution. The very core of humanistic thought is the self-actualization principle, which is an act of unfolding of the highest order. The human being is also a human becoming, and cultivation of this process is of the utmost importance in its profound and far-reaching implications.

Implicit in the metaphors of man as mechanism and man as organism is the ultimate epistemological principle of man as that which *knows* mechanism and organism. We speak here of the knowing Subject or conscious Self, the experiencer or witness to all that is experienced. As a particular viewpoint or manifestation of the Infinite Consciousness, it is the ever-present moment, the here-and-now, the living Spirit that knows and creates its object, the finite world, through an act of selfless abandon and love.

When man as spirit is not part of our definition and understanding of the nature of man, we treat him as a strictly psychological and physical being. Jung took a step toward articulating this third principle by positing the archetypes, including the Self, as transpersonal, or transcendent of the individual order. Yet the conscious Self, as a manifestation of the Infinite Consciousness, transcends not only the individual order but the finite order as well. Perhaps Maslow came closest to this point by considering the humanistic model in terms of its own limitations. Recognizing that there is more to human nature than the psychophysical process of self-actualization per se, he made reference to the spiritual aspects of human experience that transcend self-actualization and cannot be described in its own terms.

If psychotherapy is to be any kind of vehicle for spiritual liberation, the Spirit or conscious Self must be integral to our understanding and experience of our own human nature or ontology. In its essential infinitude the Spirit hungers not. It does not need an object, because needs are based on deficits, and the Infinite can never be deficient in any way. To the contrary, with inestimable and unfathomable repletion, it gives or surrenders itself to the object, and in this act of selfless love creates the finite world. When the Self is aware of its principle infinitude and transcendence, the movement of love is unitive, and form is cultivated. When the Self is unconsciously identified with all that it knows and loves, specifically the empirical ego, it experiences the fear and insecurity of finitude, and the movement of love becomes separative.

It is thus that the essence of the spiritual life, or the free movement of the Spirit, lies in the cultivation of the individuality of form. When form is organic, the act of cultivation is the facilitation of its outward volution, or the unfolding of form qua form, along the lines of its given nature. Under the best circumstances, when the organic form is the seed of human being and personality, the act of cultivation begins at birth, and becomes a way of life. A dialectical relationship is forged with the child, and the foundation for freedom is established. More typically, human form is not cultivated but subjugated, as the innate movement toward outward volution, as an act of freedom, is obstructed and subverted by the didactic process. The spiritual life is lost or never discovered, and the life so lived is dictated by, and expressive of, the separative movement of the universe.

When the conscious Self or Spirit is not integral to our understanding of man, we proceed accordingly. Human suffering is diagnosed as either physical or psychological, for we are not more than psychophysical beings. The treatment of these diagnoses depends on whether man is a mechanism or an organism. When man is mechanistic, he must be fixed or corrected. When man is organismic, he must be allowed to heal. *Medicus curat, natura sanat.* "The doctor treats, nature heals."

As noted, the cognitive, behavioral, and psychoanalytic approaches to human disorder view man mechanistically, and treat him as such. Maladaptive thoughts and behaviors are modified and corrected as new cognitive-behavioral structures are learned, conditioned, and reinforced. There is no conception or concern for liberating the dialectical process, since man is a soulless mechanism that must operate efficiently and in accordance with socially constructed guidelines. The Jungian, interpersonal, and client-centered approaches, in their organismic view of man, do not look to fix the individual, but rather set the conditions for growth and healing. There is an implied faith in the innate wisdom of the organism, and absolute justification of the process of outward volution or unfolding as the cardinal principle of freedom and health.

The importance of the organismic model is that it implies the Spirit, in its emphasis on the cultivation of individuality. The very notion of individuation or self-actualization clearly holds that the given form is sacred, and that the process of articulation is both intelligent and meaningful. Whether in the form of healthy developmental nurturance or psychotherapy, the cultivation of form takes an act of love or selfless abandon, which is the movement of the liberated Spirit to liberate the Spirit in the form. Jung's Self, being an archetype, is not properly psychological in nature, for it transcends individuality and objective knowledge. Maslow came closer to the principle of transcending finitude and not simply individuality by placing spiritual needs at the pinnacle of his hierarchy, beyond description or explanation in the psychophysical terms of self-actualization.

Although the organismic model implies the Spirit, we cannot avoid the practical question of whether the relevant therapies actually fulfill the ultimate psychotherapeutic objective of liberating the dialectical process. This is not to say that this objective must be articulated as such theoretically, or expressly intended therapeutically, in order to be actualized in the course of therapy. It can just as easily be effected implicitly and indirectly. Yet the measure of this effect is discernible. We exemplified the personality of the liberated Spirit as dialectically free, and thus interpersonally and vocationally fulfilled. Spiritual enrichment issues in personal happiness and joy, and a wondrous absence of developmental stagnation. We noted that with ongoing growth and unfolding there is a rich and utterly replete subjective life. Since it is in the nature of repletion to spill or run over, it is quite natural for the individual to give selflessly, with a pure outpouring of love that touches the minds and hearts of those who come in contact with him. His inner peace, naturalness, and refreshing absence of self-justification and militant theism make those in his presence feel comfortable and open.

In considering the organismic therapies we may look for these qualities as a measure of their success. There is potential benefit from all forms of psychotherapy, but we refer quite specifically to the liberation of the dialectical process. Laborious and unsystematized though it may be, it is perhaps a more profitable method of study to proceed on a case-by-case basis. In the same way that psychoanalytic patients can become "Freudianized," Jungian patients can become "Jungianized." To the degree that one is "ized" by a psychotherapeutic process, one has not individuated. The very point is not to "stamp" the individual in any way. Moreover, profiles of Maslow's self-actualizers often show them to be petulant and self-absorbed people, not necessarily happy, and not the best company. Apparently, the development of talents and interests in itself does not carry the same personal maturity as when this development is part of a larger process of psychoemotional growth.

Psychological sculpting, as a therapeutic technique, moves explicitly and directly to liberate the dialectical process. We described this technique as subtractive and akin to sculpting in stone, for the intrinsic form, in its absolute purity, is to be revealed and not effected. By first rendering the didactic introject visible through objectification and identification (what is being said and who is saying it), and then transparent by releasing its hold on dialectical thought, we introduce an unprecedented freedom into the life of the individual. Discerning his own talents and aptitudes, formulating his own interests and ideas, the individual discovers his "original face," or the reality of his being, as it is a given in the finite world. With clear consciousness of who he is, and a proper measure of loving support, he can begin to unfold, authentically and from his center of being, enjoying the richness and fulfillment of a life that is tapped from its nethermost roots. In a manner more profound and compelling than intellectual articulation, he understands the fundamental identity of the psychological and the spiritual. It becomes an intimate fact of experience that the dialectical process *is* the free movement of the Spirit, and that this movement, as an act of selfless love, tends to the perfection of the finite order by developing it in accordance with its limitations, or cultivating the individuality of its forms.

The beauty and elegance of the principle of outward volution, as the cultivation of organic form, lies in its freedom and truth, and the unique nature of its temporality. As that which unfolds, or turns itself inside out, what manifests later in time is progressively of a more central and fundamental nature. This challenges the more traditional Western conceptions of maturation and aging as somehow reaching a peak or plateau, and then progressively declining. As he continues to age, the individual wanes and dissipates, like the artist who is "just tapped out." The sociology of aging is so powerful that he will devalue himself, as he is devalued by others, for being older, and frequently use the phrase "in my day," as if his day somehow passed. Yet if he is still alive, when did it officially end?

With outward volution, when it is cultivated, *today* is one's day, always with the titillating but nondistracting intimation that the best is yet to come. Unfolding before us is intelligent form, articulating, expressing, and evolving. Unfolding from its center of being, turning itself inside out, the nature of its temporality is a gift. Time is not cursed for its ravages, but cherished as the precious medium for ongoing manifestations of individuality of increasing profundity and meaning. The freedom and truth that inhere in this act of outward volution underscore the reality that the life so lived is *willed* and not determined, and therefore never subject to futility and despair.

When the Spirit is integral to our understanding and experience of ourselves, we know that we are more than psychophysical beings. The psychophysical being is finite, an object of knowledge, for we discover that we are also the conscious Self that knows this psychophysical being. Conceived as a mechanism, the psychophysical being is meant to function efficiently. As an organism, it is meant to individuate. Since there is little joy and freedom in efficient functioning if this functioning has no personal significance, addressing human disorder, with the understanding of man as spirit, cannot then be a philosophy of fixing from without, but must be one of facilitating from within. Since the organismic model implies the Spirit, the arena of human suffering predicated on the obstruction of outward volution is ultimately a manifestation of spiritual disease.

As intelligent organicity, the psychophysical being knows its path, for it is the path with heart. The movement to heal is the same as the movement to unfold, and in its social context it needs the selfless love of others and oneself. Burgeoning from its center of being, the human form is known to, or loved by, the conscious Self or Spirit. In this fact of existential authenticity lies the purpose and meaning of life, for it is the incarnation of Infinite Being. In every moment of its being and becoming it mirrors eternity, and thus it is eternally significant. It is therefore meaningless to seek the spiritual life in another place and time, for it is to be *realized*, with eminent clarity, *here and now*, as the unitive movement of love, moving with form it its ongoing articulation and expression. Tending to our own perfection, we tend to a divine likeness, for each instance of pure individuality is the finite manifestation or "image" of Infinite Being and Consciousness, knowing itself as such, and loving selflessly in the creation of the universe.

References

Ajzen, I. 1988. *Attitudes, Personality and Behavior*. Chicago: Dorsey Press.

Asaad, G. 1996. *Psychosomatic Disorders: Theoretical and Clinical Aspects*. New York: Brunner-Mazel.

Asch, S. E. 1951. Effects of group pressure upon the modification and distortion of judgment. In *Groups, Leadership and Men*, edited by H. Guetzkow. Pittsburgh: Carnegie Press.

Beck, A. T. 1976. *Cognitive Therapy and the Emotional Disorders*. Madison: International Universities Press.

Berger, P. L., and T. Luckmann 1966. *The Social Construction of Reality*. New York: Anchor Books.

Bowers, K. S. 1984. On being unconsciously influenced and informed. In *The Unconscious Revisited*, edited by K. S. Bowers and D. Meichenbaum. New York: John Wiley.

Breuer, J., and S. Freud (1895.) Studies on hysteria. In *The Standard Edition of the Complete Psychological Works of Sigmund Freud*, edited by J. Strachey. Vol. 2. London: Hogarth Press, 1955.

Capra, F. 1975. *The Tao of Physics*. Berkeley: Shambhala.

Castaneda, C. 1968. *The Teachings of Don Juan: A Yaqui Way of Knowledge*. Chicago: University of Chicago Press.

Cooley, C. H. 1902. *Human Nature and Social Order*. New York: Scribner.

Dollard, J., and N. Miller 1950. *Personality and Psychotherapy*. New York: McGraw Hill.

Eaves, L., H. J. Eysenck and N. G. Martin 1989. *Genetics, Culture and Personality*. New York: Academic Press.

Erdelyi, M. H. 1985. *Psychoanalysis: Freud's Cognitive Psychology*. New York: Freeman.

Erdelyi, M. H., and B. Goldberg 1977. Let's not sweep repression under the rug: Toward a cognitive psychology of repression. In *Functional Disorders of Memory*, edited by J. F. Kihlstrom and F. J. Evans. Hillsdale: Lawrence Erlbaum.

Eysenck, H. J. 1967. *The Biological Bases of Personality*. Springfield: Thomas.

Fishbein, M., and I. Ajzen 1975. *Belief, Attitude, Intention and Behavior: An Introduction to Theory and Research*. Reading: Addison Wesley Press.

Freud, S. (1912.) A note on the unconscious in psychoanalysis. In *The Standard Edition of the Complete Psychological Works of Sigmund Freud*, edited by J. Strachey. Vol. 12. London: Hogarth Press, 1957.

Freud, S. (1914.) On narcissism: An introduction. In *The Standard Edition of the Complete Psychological Works of Sigmund Freud*, edited by J. Strachey. Vol. 14. London: Hogarth Press, 1957.

Freud, S. (1915a.) Repression. In *The Standard Edition of the Complete Psychological Works of Sigmund Freud*, edited by J. Strachey. Vol. 14. London: Hogarth Press, 1957.

Freud, S. (1915b.) The unconscious. In *The Standard Edition of the Complete Psychological Works of Sigmund Freud*, edited by J. Strachey. Vol. 14. London: Hogarth Press, 1957.

Freud, S. (1917.) Mourning and melancholia. In *The Standard Edition of the Complete Psychological Works of Sigmund Freud*, edited by J. Strachey. Vol. 14. London: Hogarth Press, 1957.

Freud, S. (1920.) Beyond the pleasure principle. In *The Standard Edition of the Complete Psychological Works of Sigmund Freud*, edited by J. Strachey. Vol. 18. London: Hogarth Press, 1961.

Freud, S. (1923.) The ego and the id. In *The Standard Edition of the Complete Psychological Works of Sigmund Freud*, edited by J. Strachey. Vol. 19. London: Hogarth Press, 1961.

Freud, S. (1924.) The dissolution of the Oedipus-complex. In *The Standard Edition of the Complete Psychological Works of Sigmund Freud*, edited by J. Strachey. Vol. 19. London: Hogarth Press, 1961.

Freud, S. (1926.) Inhibitions, symptoms and anxiety. In *The Standard Edition of the Complete Psychological Works of Sigmund Freud*, edited by J. Strachey. Vol. 20. London: Hogarth Press, 1964.

Freud, S. (1933.) New introductory lectures on Psychoanalysis. In *The Standard Edition of the Complete Psychological Works of Sigmund Freud*, edited by J. Strachey. Vol. 20. London: Hogarth Press, 1964.

Goffman, E. 1959. *The Presentation of Self in Everyday Life*. New York: Anchor Books.

Guthrie, A. 1967. *Alice's Restaurant*. New York: Warner Reprise Records.

Harlow, H. F., and C. M. Harlow 1986. *From Learning to Love: The Selected Papers of H. F. Harlow*. New York: Praeger.

Heidegger, M. (1927.) *Being and Time*. Translated by J. Stambaugh. Albany: State University of New York Press, 1953.

Husserl, E. (1913.) *Ideas: General Introduction to Pure Phenomenology*. Translated by W. R. Boyce Gibson. London: George Allen and Unwin, Ltd., 1931.

Jagger, M., and K. Richards 1969. You can't always get what you want. *Let It Bleed*. London: Decca Records.

Jung, C. G. (1928.) Two essays on analytical psychology. In *The Collected Works of C. G. Jung,* edited by H. Read, M. Fordham, and G. Adler. Vol. 7. Princeton: Princeton University Press, 1953.

Jung, C. G. (1934.) The archetypes of the collective unconscious. In *The Collected Works of C. G. Jung,* edited by H. Read, M. Fordham, and G. Adler. Vol. 9. Princeton: Princeton University Press, 1959.

Kierkegaard, S. (1846.) *Concluding Unscientific Postscript.* Translated by D. F. Swenson and W. Lawrence. Princeton: Princeton University Press, 1941.

Kuhn, T. 1962. *The Structure of Scientific Revolutions.* Chicago: University of Chicago Press.

Laing, R. D. 1972. *The Politics of the Family.* London: Vintage.

Lazarus, A. A. 1971. *Behavior Therapy and Beyond.* New York: McGraw-Hill.

Levenson, J. L. 2006. *Essentials of Psychosomatic Medicine.* Arlington: American Psychiatric Press.

Maslow, A. 1954. *Motivation and Personality.* New York: Harper.

Maslow, A. 1962. *Toward a Psychology of Being.* New York: Van Nostrand.

Mead, G. H. 1934. *Mind, Self and Society.* Chicago: University of Chicago Press.

Nims, J. F. 1998. *The Complete Poems of Michelangelo.* Chicago: University of Chicago Press.

Piaget, J. 1952. *The Origins of Intelligence in Children.* New York: International Universities Press.

Plomin, R., and G. E. McClearn 1993. *Nature, Nurture and Psychology.* Washington DC: American Psychological Association.

Plutchik, R. 1980. *Emotion: A Psychoevolutionary Synthesis.* New York: Harper and Row.

Provence, S., and R. C. Lipton 1962. *Infants in Institutions.* New York: International Universities Press.

Rogers, C. R. 1951. *Client-Centered Therapy: Its Current Practice, Implications and Theory.* Boston: Houghton Mifflin.

Sartre, J. P. (1943.) *Being and Nothingness: A Phenomenological Essay on Ontology.* Translated by H. Barnes. London: Routledge, 1957.

Seinfeld, J. 1990. *The Bad Object.* New Jersey: Jason Aronson.

Silverman, L. H. 1983. The subliminal psychodynamic activation method: Overview and comprehensive listing of studies. In *Empirical Studies of Psychoanalytic Theories,* edited by J. Masling. Hillsdale: Lawrence Erlbaum.

Spotnitz, H. 1985. *Modern Psychoanalysis of the Schizophrenic Patient: Theory of the Technique.* New York: Human Sciences Press.

Stills, S. 1970. Love the one you're with. *Stephen Stills.* New York: Atlantic Records.

Sullivan, H. S. 1953. *The Interpersonal Theory of Psychiatry.* New York: Norton.

Suzuki, D. T. 1949. *Essays in Zen Buddhism.* London: Ryder and Company.

Suzuki, D. T. 1956. *Zen Buddhism.* New York: Anchor Books.

Thomas, I., and S. Chess 1977. *Temperament and Development.* New York: Brunner-Mazel.

Washington, J. M. 1990. *A Testament of Hope: The Essential Writings and Speeches of Martin Luther King Jr.* New York: HarperOne.

Watts, A. W. 1948. *The Supreme Identity.* London: Wildwood House.

Watts, A. W. 1957. *The Way of Zen.* New York: Random House.

About the Author

Dr. Ben Goldberg holds a doctorate in Personality Psychology and is a Licensed Clinical Social Worker. His career has been academically and clinically diverse. On the academic side he served as Assistant Professor of Psychology and Adjunct Lecturer at several colleges and universities in the New York City area, as well as Research Psychologist for the New York City Police Department. On the clinical side he worked as a staff psychotherapist and literary contributor to a number of mental-health facilities and psychotherapy training institutes in New York, and for five years was a principle consultant to New York Telephone (now Verizon), where he provided short-term stress-management therapy, and conducted managerial training seminars and communications-analysis and conflict-resolution workshops for corporate executives.

Ben has been in private practice for the past twenty-five years. During this time he founded Personality Concepts, which is a consulting group providing psychological services to individuals, couples and families, as well as small businesses and corporations. Ben has developed a theoretical and practical model of psychotherapy that holds sacred the fundamental uniqueness of the individual.

Aside from psychology, Ben's passions are philosophy, theology, sociology, literature, rock drumming, and mostly his wonderful wife and two beautiful sons. He currently resides in Rockville Centre, New York.